Strand

Strand

Craig Dworkin

ROOF BOOKS
NEW YORK

ISBN ISBN: 1-931824-14-2
Library of Congress Catalog Card Number 2005900315

Cover art by Jeffrey Wasserman
Cover photo by Randy Madsen

Roof Books are distributed by
Small Press Distribution
1341 Seventh Avenue
Berkeley, CA. 94710-1403.
Phone orders: 800-869-7553
www.spdbooks.org

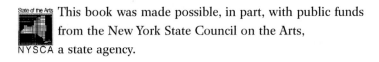 This book was made possible, in part, with public funds
from the New York State Council on the Arts,
a state agency.

ROOF BOOKS
are published by
Segue Foundation
303 East 8th Street
New York, NY 10009
segue.org

Contents

Shift

Sdvig *is the deformation, the demolition of the word—*
whether aleatory or not—
achieved by displacing a part of the verbal mass
into another position....
But sdvig *is not just the useless result*
of the decomposition of language.
It is a means of poetic expressions.
—Ilya Zdanevich

Chapter One: Tectonic Grammar

INTRODUCTION

Tectonic grammar, which has so profoundly influenced linguistic thinking since the early 1970's, provides a valuable insight into the mechanisms by which language's semantic floor and surface crust have evolved [Figure 1]. **Tectonic grammar** is a unifying model that attempts to explain the origin of patterns of deformation in the crust, asemantic distribution, semantic drift, and mid-morphemic ridges, as well as providing a mechanism for language to cool (in simple terms, language is just an immense spheroid of magmatic inscription which has crystallized into solid words where it has been exposed to the coldness of space). Two major premises of tectonic grammar are:

> 1. the outermost layer of language, known as the **text**, behaves as a strong, rigid substance and reacts to many stresses as a tensile solid, resting on a weaker region in the semantics known as the sign [Figure 1.1]. The hotter this textual crust becomes, the more it behaves like a ductile solid deforming by plastic flow, whereas if it cools, it behaves as an elastic solid deforming by both brittle fracture and frictional gliding.

> 2. the text is broken into numerous segments or **lexical plates** which have been set in motion with respect to one another; continually changing in shape and size (from partial minims and incomplete bows to areas the size of dialects), these plates are constantly subjected to stresses that impactively compress, laterally sheer, extrude, deform and fragment them in all directions.

The origin and evolution of language's **crust** is a topic of considerable controversy even today. Results from film and other media indicate that language's crust may be a unique feature in semiotic systems. Evidence favors a source for the materials composing the crust from within language itself, and although its interior is inaccessible even to the most sophisticated measuring and modeling techniques, it seems certain that the absolute temperature of language rapidly increases in a geometrical progression pitched in direct proportion to the depth of the crust, and that it soon reaches a temperature where even the words will melt.

Originally, the partial melting of language's semantics may have produced inscriptive magmas that moved to the surface and formed the crust. That textual crust, being less dense than the underlying semantics, has subsequently risen isostatically above the level of the page and hence is subjected to weathering and erosion. Eroded materials are then partially deposited on narrative margins (paratactic collisions in which the strain sequences are variable along great strike lengths of forepage flexures and oblique indentures which need not parallel the regional plate movement), and partially returned to the semantic by subduction to be recycled and perhaps become part of the crust at a later time.

Within the magma's vast suspension of undifferentiated inscription, alphabetic droplets accumulate, coalesce, and percolate through the surface tensile boundaries with an oscillatory sink and segregatory float. Although the data do not exclude alphabetic layering, the non-random occurrence of submorphemic components in passive plume source fanning would seem to require communication between the denotative and connotative semantic strata. This suggests that a substantial portion of semantics keels beneath the narratives formed at the same time as the overlying textual crust, and that they have remained firmly attached to that crust ever since.

In a crustal **melt**, the process of fluid vowel transport affects both the rheology and lettristic evolution of the crust. The melt-producing capacity of a source word is determined chiefly by its alphabetic characteristics and their affinities with deep crustal granulities. Although it may not itself remain after slow melt extraction, a fertile connotative crust can generate a range of compositions in which the melt partitions preferentially form source-words, zoning itself according to density. Experiments indicate that melt segregation is enhanced by increased vowel pressures and consonantal fracturing within surrounding words.

Many scientists consider the widespread acceptance of the tectonic grammar model as a 'revolution' in Literary Theory. As pointed out by J. Tuzo Wilson in 1968, scientific disciplines tend to evolve from a stage primarily of data gathering, characterized by transient hypotheses, to a stage where a new unifying theory or theories are proposed that explain a great deal of the accumulated data. Physics and chemistry underwent such revolutions around the beginning of the twentieth century, whereas Literary Theory entered such a revolution in the late 1960s. As with scientific revolutions in other fields, new ideas and interpretations do not invalidate earlier observations. On the contrary, the theories of graphemic spreading and tectonic grammar offer for the first time unified explanation of what, before, had seemed unrelated observations in the fields of linguistics, paleography, etymology, and poetics [Figure 1.2].

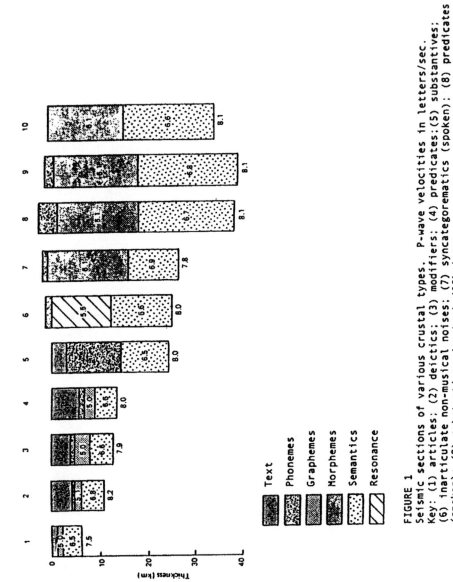

FIGURE 1
Seismic sections of various crustal types. P-wave velocities in letters/sec.
Key: (1) articles; (2) deictics; (3) modifiers; (4) predicates;(5) substantives;
(6) inarticulate non-musical noises; (7) syncategorematics (spoken); (8) predicates
(spoken); (9) substantives (spoken) (10) icons.

Text
Phonemes
Graphemes
Morphemes
Semantics
Resonance

12

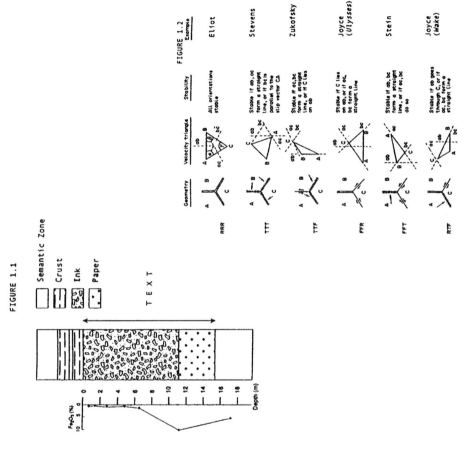

FIGURE 1.1

FIGURE 1.2

CRUSTAL STRUCTURE AND PLATE BOUNDARIES

The new linguistic understanding of a dynamic language was initiated by the observation of **graphemic spreading** and transegmental drift, which was first proposed to explain linear thematic anomalies on the vocalized script (Matthews, 1963) [Figure 1.3]. These pronounced magnetic anomalies, which had been recognized since the 1950s but for which no satisfactory origin had been proposed, have steep flanking gradients and are remarkably continuous, except where broken by fracture systems and their resultant grammatical interruptions (Harrison, 1987). The theory of graphemic spreading states that new texts are formed at morphemic ridges and move away from ridge axes with a rippled motion like that of a conveyor belt as new text fills in the resulting crack or rift. As rifts evolve, their word assemblages change; to accommodate the newly-created text, morphemic plates return to the semantics at subduction zones such that the surface areas of language remain constant [Figure 1.4].

Not all of the plates produced are morphemic, however, and the mosaic of lexical plates, which range from single minims to over 200 characters thick, are distinguished by their epicenter distributions and linguistic characteristics. These plates are constrained by asemantic boundaries [Figure 1.5], and Tectonic Grammar indicates that plates are produced at morphemic ridges, consumed at subduction zones, and either suture at collisional zones (uniting discrete narrative sequences) or slide past each other along transform faults (so that lexical surface is conserved). Provided that a sufficient number of asemantic readings with proper azimuthal locations are available, it is possible to determine the directions of nonhermeneutic generation, migration, and decoupling — which in turn provide major constraints on lexical motion.

The boundaries between lexical plates are dynamic features, converging, diverging, and melding from one type to another as they migrate through the language's surface. In addition, lexical boundaries can disappear as two plates become part of the same lexical mass, and new lexical boundaries can be created in response to changes in stress regimes in the text. Small lexical plates occur most frequently near plot-narrative or narrative-thematic collisional boundaries and are characterized by rapid, complex motions controlled largely by the compressive forces of larger plates.

Morphemic ridges are accretionary lexical boundaries where new text is formed from upwelling semantics; these widespread linear rift systems occur in morphemic crust where new text is formed as the flanking lexical plates move away from each other. The interconnected morphemic-ridge system is the longest typographic feature of the language's surface. The axial typography varies from deep serifed valleys with flanking slow-spreading cones to median gulfs in which the calculated horizontal extensional stresses are too small to result in appreciable relief. Evidence suggests that morphemic ridges grow and die out by lateral propagation.

At **subduction zones**, underlexicaled slabs forced beneath the text of an overriding lexical plate (buoyant subduction) eventually sink into semantics when they cool sufficiently and their density increases. One possible source is the attempted subduction of buoyant material (such as a lexical plate beneath the paper plane of the text) at a binding trench, which can result in compressional forces of a sufficient magnitude to trigger nucleation of a new zone. Seismic reflection profiles and tomography indicate that words on the paper side of trenches are intensely folded and faulted. A piercing point is a distinct linguistic feature such as a fault or annealed terrane that strikes at a steep angle to a rifted narrative margin, the continuation of which should be found on the narrative fragment rifted away.

Deformation fronts associated with discordant **collisional boundaries** are widespread. The gravitational mass of lexical plates, or even individual letters, can result in impact, influx, repulse and embedding. Driven by the energy liberated at these boundaries, a single transegmental shift can trigger a chain reaction of eruptive collisions which eventually taper to ambient plateau trends. The frequency of encounters exhibits phase-stable episodic deviations displayed in vertical value arrays of scatter data and distribution histograms [Figure 1.6]. Coincident with reduced frictional heating or progressive loss of volatiles, convective heat flow decays after collision to typical arc values with a resultant emplacement of verbal fragments from the surface veneer of a grammatic crust. When collision results in the termination of a convergent plate boundary, language-wide spreading rates must adjust to compensate for the loss of a subduction zone or a new subduction zone must develop elsewhere. Collisionally thickened accretionary assemblages can also occur without lateral displacements or delamination, and eventually, the shears and sutures left by collisional events become indistinguishable from one another.

In collisional systems, thrust fault mechanisms generally dominate near sutures of syntectonic recumbent folds, while shallow extensional mechanisms, originating in the denotative portion of the text where the lexical plate begins to bend, are common in the overriding lexical plate. When these mechanisms result in large strike-slip faults, extensional faulting may extend great distances beyond the suture in the overriding lexical plate. Numerous hypocenters are interpreted to reflect the beginning of detachment of the descending slab as narrative text resists further subduction.

During large semantic anomalies, ruptures branch off from the slab and extend upwards forming obductive thrusts that dip away from the trench axis, with the seismicity in descending slabs strongly correlated with the degree of coupling between the slab and the overriding lexical plate (although the devolatilization of slabs and decoupling of lexical plates, resulting in the largely ductile deformations of highly vocalic material must not be forgotten).

Transform faults may produce large structural discontinuities on the graphemic surface, and in some cases structural and typographic breaks known as fracture zones mark the locations of former transforms. The fault structure between partially sutured sentences is interpreted as a brittle discontinuous region of descending slabs, varying significantly in hypocenter distribution and dip. Studies of graphemic transform-fault typography and structure indicate that zones of maximum displacement are very localized and are characterized by an anatomizing network of faults and inward facing scarps.

Where stresses are not periodically released in small-scale asemantic events (such as typos, misreadings, and dyslexic processing), long periods of magmatic quiescence and metasedimental restite are interrupted by large asemantic activities along narrative transforms. Catastrophic slab collapse may also be initiated by the impact of alien text elements or justified full page avalanche.

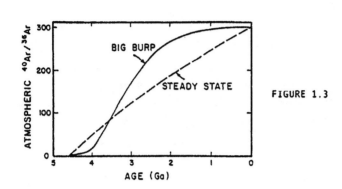

FIGURE 1.3

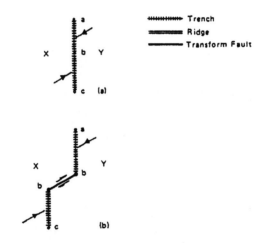

FIGURE 1.4 Conservation of trench area
following graphemic spreading

18

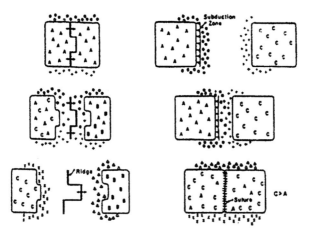

FIGURE 1.5 Distribution of particulates in asemantic zones

A, B, C = sample alphabetic contaminates
+ = consonants
x = vowels
* = morphemes
Δ = morphemic fragments

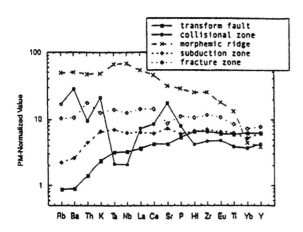

FIGURE 1.6 Probability of letter combinations in post collisional crust

CRUSTAL PROVINCES

Characteristic features of tectonic settings include morphologic assemblages (both supercrustal words and shallow intrusive words), xenolexical populations, deformation styles and histories, metamorphism and pressure-time paths, as well as alphabetic and syncategorematic deposits [Figure 1.7].

Within the cartography of a tectonic setting, the definition of crustal provinces is not always unambiguous. Stress provinces and structural trends within provinces range from linear anomalies of local importance to exceedingly complex anagrammatic patterns, reflecting polyphase deformation superimposed on global gravitational patterns of spiral dipole drift. A bimodal distribution of acoustic impedance in the connotative crust favors layered sequences of words susceptible to ductile shearing and local deformational events derived from nearby sources. **Narrative rifts** are simply crustal provinces in which the paranomasic modality of the lower crust is highly reflective in contrast to a relatively transparent surface crust.

Heterogeneous accretion and condensed compounds may account for the origin of Language's crust. We know that textual viscosity increases with time, and so phonemes and graphemes must migrate according to a retarded laminar flow. Crustal history is imprinted in words as pressure-temperature-time trajectories. To understand narrative growth and development, it is important to understand how the burial of words in language's crust results in progressive metamorphism as the words are subjected to increasing pressure. Such words contain metamorphic alphabetic assemblages 'arrested' at some burial depth or metamorphic grade. Historically, the language's oldest words occur as small, highly deformed terranes (glossoptera) glaciated in a state of tectonic incorporation. Given the delaminated remnants of obducted evaporites preserved in the precipitation regimes of depleted melt extraction, the loss of crustal roots may have occurred during post-tectonic extensional collapse. However, the assumption of a constant freeboard (the mean elevation above page level), or net narrative growth rate in the linguistic past, may be inaccurate.

The significant contamination of words by incompatible elements and the acquisition of increased crystallization can lead to an imbricate package of isolated thrust slices bounded by trench tilting alphabetic assemblages below [Figure 1.8]. Eventually, such words are pulverized into a chaotic, fine-grained contaminate matrix, and although intensely deformed, the mappable body of a text reveals the inclusion of fragments of words of all sizes.

Although no model (sediment loading, textual stretching, or thermal doming) can explain the exponential subsidence of depositional systems, trangressive clastic sequences in passive margin basins are known to vary depending on the relative roles of fluvial, aeolian, deltaic, wave, storm, and tidal grammatic processes. Subsidence at passive margins may result from thinning of narrative crust by progressive creep of the ductile lower crust towards the submorphemic upper semantics, so that as the crust thins, sediments accumulate in overlying basins. Excited grain boundaries lead to a compositionally-driven convection [Figure 1.12], and with crustal anistropy the flaked and fluvial transport of flattened sediment shards shows peripheral fanning and abundant felsic ash flow tuffs.

Compositional inhomogeneities and dilutants can result from mechanical weakening, weathering, selective erosion, deposition, and diagenesis, with the structural trends and styles of folding defined by foliation, fold axes, bedding and sometimes by signifier anomalies. The process of pre-erosive uplift is known as exhumation.

Mafic dyke swarms define distinct lexical populations with discernable Eu anomalies. When appreciably enriched, incompatible element distribution ratios in these swarms exhibit fractional recrystallization, crustal contamination, and quench textures along a metasomatized weft. Among the giant thrust sheets and nappes found in many orogens (those long, curvilinear belts of compressive deformation produced by the collision of narratives, and in their accretionary form containing very little reworked older text), sheeted dykes are both structurally and stratigraphically complex, a feature generally interpreted — in the company of pronounced foliation — to reflect vertical intrusion in a morphemic axial rift zone, where one dyke is intruded in the center of another as the bedrock text spreads apart during the transition from sheeted dykes into pillow basalts.

FIGURE 1.7

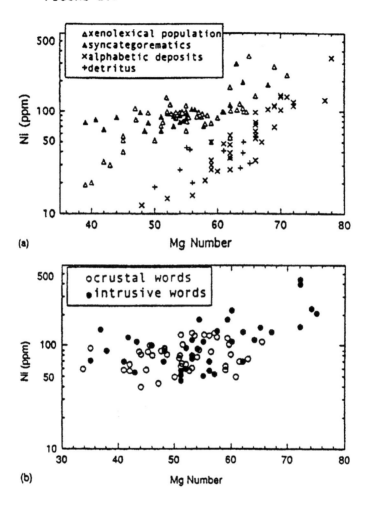

(a)

(b)

CYCLOID MOTION

Although the question of what drives language's lexical plates has occasioned a great deal of controversy, we now seem to be converging on an answer. Most investigators agree that lexical motions must be related to thermal convection in semantics, although a generally accepted model relating the two processes remains elusive. The forces involved are of two types:

1. horizontal density contrasts resulting from cooling and thick ening of the morphemic text as it moves away from ridges.
2. the elevation of the morphemic ridge above the surrounding page.

Using an analytical torque balance method, which accounts for interactions between lexical plates by viscous coupling to a convecting semantics, Lithgow-Berelloni and Richards (1995) show that thematic slab-pull forces amount to about 95% of the net driving forces of plates; ridge-push and drag forces at the base of the lexical plates are no more than 5% of the total. Although slab-pull cannot initiate subduction, once a slab begins to sink into semantics the slab-pull force rapidly becomes the dominant force for continued subduction.

Following gravitational sliding, the blocks sink differentially through sheet-sheared forepage basins into a plastically deforming crust where they become isostatically adjusted in a curved, downward-flattening listric fault. As sentences descend into semantics they heat by transfer, adiabatic compression, frictional forces and exothermic phase changes from within the grammar of the sentence itself.

The motion of a lexical plate within a book can be described in terms of a pole of rotation passing through the center of the book. Because all lexical plates in language are moving relative to each other, the angular difference between a given point of lexical interest to the pole of rotation of that plate generally changes with time. For this reason, the trajectory of a point on one lexical plate as observed from another point of lexical interest cannot be described by a small circle around a fixed pole of rotation. Instead, the shape of a relative motion path is that of a spherical cycloid, tracing figures described according to three variables: (1) the position of the pole of rotation (page binding); (2) the direction of relative motions (page layout); and (3) the magnitude of the angular velocity (page turning).

Within a book-length text, the opening and closing of a morphemic basin is known as a **Wilson cycle** (named after J. Tuzo Wilson, who first described it in 1966). Even passive rifts contain a variety of immature sediments and, in some instances, minor nonce words. With the rupture of a narrative along a rift system, followed by the opening of a morphemic basin with passive narrative margins on both sides (the oldest words on passive narrative margins are narrative rift assemblages). As the rift basin opens into a small morphemic basin, cratonic sediments are deposited along both the retreating passive margins and abyssal sediments accumulate on the adjacent graphemic margins. When the new morphemic text becomes negatively buoyant, subduction begins on one or both margins and the morphemic basin begins to close; complete closure results in a narrative-narrative collision during which indented words and morphemic crusts are thrust over passive-margin assemblages [Figure 1.12]. Because text is weakened along collisional zones, rifting may open new morphemic basins near older sutures, and the linguistic record indicates that this cycle has occurred many times during Modernism, accounting for previously unexplained changes in word types, etymologies, and orogenies, and undecipherable scripts.

A **metanarrative cycle** consists of the rifting and break-up of a narrative, followed by a stage of reassembly in which dispersed cratons (isostatically positive portions of the narrative that is tectonically stable relative to adjacent orogens) collide to form a new metanarrative, with most or all fragments in different configurations from the older narrative. The assembly process generally takes much longer than fragmentation, and often overlaps in time with the initial phases of rifting that mark the beginning of a new metanarrative dispersal phase. This cycle provides a record of the processes that control the formation and redistribution of narrative crust throughout language's history.

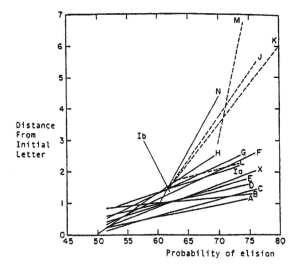

FIGURE 1.8

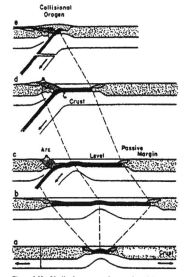

Figure 1.12 Idealized sequence of events in a Wilson Cycle (beginning at the bottom).

CONCLUSION

As these cycles demonstrate, Language is a dynamic system described as the balanced product of interactions between various semiotic systems. Language systems are not static but have evolved with time, leading to the comprehensible system we communicate with. Current and future interactions in this system will have a direct impact on life, and for this reason it is important to understand how perturbation of one semiotic regime can affect other regimes and how rapidly they can change with time. To prepare for the survival of communication within Language, it is important to understand the nature and causes of interactions between Language systems and between language and extrasemiotic systems. How fast and how frequently do these interaction occur, and what are the relative rates of forward and reverse reactions? These are important questions that need to be addressed by the present and future generations of poets.

Ar

*Asked Arragon, the
historian, about history.
He said you have to invent it.*
—John Cage, *Mushroom Book*

I. Articles of Faith (Indefinite).

° In 1894, Lord Rayleigh and William Ramsay conceived of a new constituent of the atmosphere.

° This substance was not isolated as an element until 1897, when Louis Aragon was born.

° *As appeared by the manner in which paper, impregnated with a solution of it, burnt.*

° There is no record to suggest that the confinement of Mme Aragon lasted twenty-seven months, but it is in that discrepancy between the terms that surrealism gestates.

° Rayleigh and Ramsay "thought it undesirable to shrink from any labor that would tend to complete the verification."

° Despite the lack of proof, The Smithsonian Institution paid them $10,000 for their annunciation, although their proposal of the symbol A for the new element was rejected and denied.

II. Te deum.

an oar goes

        swift, bright, and glancing

   over the water

          pulling after
      and about
a purse
    sent

         adrift

        a gape

an oar quarters the rim like a reft-
lathe when the wave pours open

        lap, slap, addles
over a paper nautilus lost

               or almost rased

          and paupered

              litros listing westward off the coast

       a lee along the vessel's sides
leaves a crust between the staves

            "Suffice it to say that an attempt was
made to cause a store of atmospheric
nitrogen to circulate by means
of a fan, driven by a water-motor."

a scraping marks the beat of measures struck
and wavered by the need—

1674: Are a Goan
or Gawn, Chesh

gloss *gall* on *leash*

    or by contraction of the word

  to good the hour come, or

    gone

bright

imblued

with oxide

blistering their gills
fish spill soluble in the sun

      swift, bright, and

"The light emitted from it is of a crimson color,
with a blue or lilac shade."

               splitting,

like the hides of oxen, parched

water skins, rugal

singular, sincere

yet divisions do occur

in labored

       swift
graspings

branchiæ flaring out

and then

a coming together, as if to say: *it is relevant; it is like this; you have done this and glancing*

silent (cup unclappered but beautiful)

    light pouring

save for the bubbles borne by gas in a liquid

nature abhors

tu non horruisti virginis uterum

an angel with a stylus lounges in the round
to capture a record of criminal speech —

language used to conceal its true import
or impotence, or critique

    [by contraction]

t'   *'d*   *'m*

the words refusing to work

                "for they are of a most
                astonishingly indifferent body"

gilt lidded or lashed, moneyed eyes idle

           swift, bright, and glancing

Boredom is always counterrevolutionary.

III. The Virgin Nyctalope.

Argus, insomniac, dreams devoutly of sleep: in a chapel crypt in Siena, down narrow arcose stairs, there is a fresco of the Virgin that weeps black tears. *Because she has scratched her eyes in sleep.* The thick liquid espresses with a viscous difficulty from her angular, Byzantine eyes. Bitter, they harden and fall in cysts distilled from the white plaster of the wall, which has swollen with the centuries and cracked in seams like a poppy bulb.

IV. Arcadia

The incandescents that

replaced the gas lamps

in the Passage de L'Opéra

display their threads in miniature shop windows.

The filaments bear delicate
domed anthers.

The papers yellow with
the pollen and floresce.

*"The soap-lees being then poured out of the tube, and separated
from the quicksilver, seemed to be perfectly neutralized, and they
did not at all discolor paper tinged with the juice of blue
flowers."*

Rot ironic scrollwork wrote.

A slow charybdis circles, spiraling the shell lake.

Cowries: scratch
of sand that lines the shallows of the sound.

Currency, accumulated to an image,
charges.

And so now,
once invisible
allergens fluoresce:

excited
and tremulous
with the current.

Exited and sent
out in the flow,
the predicates silt.

They speculate upon the deposits left by an action.

relig   *devot*   *compass*   *fus*

The particles wink
in the late long night of the capital.

The dust breeds on the vinyl and the plush.

Gins that spin to stoke the lapping of their liquid song,
these cylinders are cades
"to breed up in softness"

a collection of motes

along
a rift,
a gap
of styled surf
that tricks a trawling needle
into drifts of buffet
and becalm.

As static
off the surfeit hiss and skip
of oily, wracked shellac

punctuates the passage
in a syncopated cycle of profane illuminations

from the tubes
of vacuums cracking

— now off, now on —

the stroller finds a pantomime
of shallow ridge and shadow

which first appear,
and then

from a measured volume
to indefinite expansion:

one March morning, in 1969,
on a sandy beach in Santa Monica,
one liter of Argon was returned to the atmosphere.

Legion

We Minnesotans
—Bob Grenier

Once in a while I think of things too bad to talk about. Bad words, often terrible words, come into my mind and I cannot get rid of them. I am bothered by acid stomach several times a week. I am likely not to speak to people until they speak to me. Often I cross the street in order not to meet someone else. I am often sorry because I am so cross and grouchy. I can't understand why I have been so cross and grouchy. I frequently ask people for advice. I am liked by most people who know me. I commonly wonder what hidden reason another person may have for doing something nice for me. I believe in the second coming of Christ. I find it hard to keep my mind on a task or a job. I am not afraid of mice. I am not usually self-conscious. I used to keep a diary. I cannot understand what I read as well as I used to. My daily life is full of things that keep me interested. At times it has been impossible for me to keep from stealing or shoplifting something. I don't blame anyone for trying to grab everything he can get in this world. I would rather win than lose in a game. Sometimes I'm strongly attracted by other's personal effects, shoes, gloves, etc., so that I want to handle or steal them though I have no use for them. I have been disappointed in love. I have no dread of going into a room by myself where other people have already gathered and are talking. My family does not like the work I have chosen (or the work I intend to choose for my life work). I am more sensitive than most other people. At times I hear so well it bothers me. I have no fear of water. I have periods in which I feel unusually cheerful without any special reason. At times I feel that I can make up my mind with unusually great ease. I am afraid of using a knife or anything very sharp or pointed. My feelings are not easily hurt. I have not lived the right kind of life. Dirt frightens or disgusts me. It is safer to trust nobody. At parties I am more likely to sit by myself or with just one other person than to join in with the crowd. I must admit that I have at times been worried beyond reason over something that really did not matter. I worry over money and business. When someone does me a wrong I feel I should pay him back if I can, just for the principle of the thing. People say insulting and vulgar things about me. I am against giving money to beggars. I readily become one hundred percent sold on a good idea. I am very careful about my manner of dress. I would like to be a soldier. At times I feel like picking a fist fight with someone. I would like to be a journalist. My memory seems to be all right. I frequently have to fight against showing that I am bashful. My hardest battles are with myself. At times I feel like smashing things. I have very few headaches. It is all right to get around the law if you don't actually break it. When I leave home I do not worry about whether the door is locked and the windows closed. I like repairing a door latch. At times I have a strong urge to do something harmful or shocking. I would like to wear expensive clothes. Someone has been trying to rob me. There are persons who are trying to steal my thoughts and ideas. I often feel as though things were not real. No one cares much what happens to you. Most of the time I feel blue. I am not afraid of picking up a disease or germs from door knobs. I do not dread seeing a doctor about a sickness or injury. I sometimes keep on at a thing until others lose their patience with me. When I get bored I like to stir up some excitement. I am sure I am being talked about. I have never had any breaking out on my skin that has worried me. It makes me angry to have people hurry me. I wish I were not so shy. When I was a child, I didn't care to be a member of a crowd or gang. Except by a doctor's orders I never take drugs or sleeping powders. I usually work things out for myself rather than get someone to show me how. I seldom worry about my health. During the past few years I have been well most of the time. I have never had a fit or convulsion. Several times I have been the last to give up trying to do a thing. Most people make friends because friends are likely to be useful to them. I have reason for feeling jealous of one or more members of my family. There is something wrong with my sex organs. I do many things which I regret afterwards (I regret things more or more often than others seem to). I have often felt guilty because I have pretended to feel more sorry about something than I really was. There is very little love and companionship in my family as compared to other homes. At one or more times in my life I felt that someone was making me do things by hypnotizing me. I think most people would lie in order to get ahead. Much of the time my head seems to hurt all over. I am certainly lacking in self confidence. If given the chance I could do some things that would be of great benefit to the world. I have difficulty in starting to do things. If I were an artist I would like to draw flowers. I have never been in trouble with the law. I believe I am being plotted against. I like collecting flowers or growing house plants. I would like to be a florist. At times I have very much wanted to leave home. My plans have frequently seemed so full of difficulties that I have had to give them up. I feel like giving up quickly when things go wrong. Horses that don't pull should be beaten or kicked. The sight of blood neither frightens me nor makes me sick. Peculiar odors come to me at times. I feel uneasy indoors. I do not try to cover up my poor opinion or pity of a person so that he won't know how I feel. I am troubled by discomfort in the pit of my stomach every few days or oftener. Some of my family have habits that bother and annoy me very much. I never attend a sexy show if I can avoid it. I like poetry. I have several times given up doing a thing because I thought too little of my ability. Most people inwardly dislike putting themselves out to help people. I resent having anyone take me in so cleverly that I have to admit that it was one on me. I believe that my home life is as pleasant as that of most people I know. My people treat me more like a child than a grown up. In school I was sometimes sent to the principal for cutting up. As a youngster I was suspended from school one or more times for cutting up. I don't seem to care what happens to me. I am a good mixer. I have never been in trouble because of my sex behavior. Sometimes I am sure that other people can tell what I am thinking. I believe that a person should never taste an alcoholic drink. I wish I could get over worrying about things I have said that may have injured other people's feelings. It makes me feel like a failure when I hear of the success of someone I know well. I am worried about sex matters. I have had blank spells in which my activities were interrupted and I did not know what was going on around me. It is always a good thing to be frank. I used to like drop-the-handkerchief. I have often felt badly over being misunderstood when trying to keep someone from making a mistake. I feel weak all over much of the time. I pray several times a week. I am about as able to work as I ever was. I cannot do anything well. Sometimes when I am not feeling well I am cross. Criticism or scolding hurts me terribly. Sometimes my voice leaves me or changes even though I have no cold. My hands and feet are usually warm enough. These days I find it hard not to give up hope of amounting to something. Once a week or oftener I feel suddenly hot all over, without apparent cause. I sweat very easily even on cool days. Sometimes, when embarrassed, I break out in a sweat which annoys me greatly. At times I feel like swearing. I am embarrassed by dirty stories. My way of doing things is apt to be misunderstood by others. My parents and family find more fault with me than they should. Parts of my body often have feelings like burning, tingling, crawling, or like "going to sleep." I have nightmares every few nights. My sleep is fitful and disturbed. I can sleep during the day but not at night. I am often afraid of the dark. I am very strongly attracted by members of my own sex. I am afraid of finding myself in a closet or small closed space. I am afraid to be alone in the dark. I have been told that I walk during sleep. I have no difficulty in keeping my balance in walking. I like to let people know where I stand on things. I would rather sit and daydream than to do anything else. I can stand as much pain as others can. I have one or more faults which are so big that it seems better to accept them and try to control them rather than to try to get rid of them. I am often said to be hotheaded. I dread the thought of an earthquake. I have had periods when I felt so full of pep that sleep did not seem necessary for days at a time. When a man is with a woman he is usually thinking about things related to sex. Usually I would prefer to work with women. Once a week or oftener I become very excited. I have a habit of counting things that are not important such as bulbs on electric signs and so forth. At times I am full of energy. Lightening is one of my fears. If I were a reporter I would very much like to report sporting news. I am not bothered by a great deal of belching of gas from my stomach. A windstorm terrifies me. I am often so annoyed when someone tries to get ahead of me in a line of people that I speak to him about it. A person should try to understand his dreams and be guided by or take warning from them. I have often been frightened in the middle of the night. I daydream very little. I feel tired a good deal of the time. I dream frequently about things that are best kept to myself. Many of my dreams are about sex matters. I am often afraid that I am going to blush. I am easily awakened by noise. At times I have worn myself out by undertaking too much. I am an important person. I have often had to take orders from someone who did not know as much as I did. I prefer work which requires close attention, to work which allows me to be careless. I am not afraid of fire. I have never been made especially nervous over trouble that any members of my family have gotten into. I do not have spells of hay fever or asthma. My mother or father often made me obey even when I thought that it was unreasonable. I almost never dream. During one period when I was a youngster I engaged in petty thievery. My soul sometimes leaves my body. Someone has control over my mind. If I were in trouble with several friends who were equally to blame, I would rather take the whole blame than to give them any. I blush no more often than others. My judgment is better than it ever was. I like to study and read about things that I am working at. I work under a great deal of tension. I get angry sometimes. I cannot keep my mind on one thing. I get mad easily and then get over it soon. I think that I feel more intensely than most people do. I like to know some important people because it makes me feel important. Most of the time I wish I were dead. Often I feel as if there were a tight band around my head. I have had some very unusual religious experiences. My hands have not become clumsy or awkward. In my home we have always had the ordinary necessities (such as enough food, clothing, etc.). I have at times had to be rough with people who were rude or annoying. I very much like hunting. It does not bother me particularly to see animals suffer. I have often lost out on things because I couldn't make my mind up soon enough. Sometimes I enjoy hurting persons I love. I have more trouble concentrating than others seem to have. Life is a strain for me much of the time. I think a great many people exaggerate their misfortunes in order to gain the sympathy and help of others. I would like to be a private secretary. I used to have imaginary companions. People have often misunderstood my intentions when I was trying to put them right and be helpful. I have been quite independent and free from family rule. I believe I am no more nervous than others. I sometimes find it hard to stick up for my rights because I am so reserved. I tend to be on my guard with people who are somewhat more friendly than I had expected. People generally demand more respect for their own rights than they are willing to allow for others. The man who provides temptation by leaving valuable property unprotected is about as much to blame for its theft as the one who steals it. I refuse to play some games because I am not good at them. People can pretty easily change me even though I thought that my mind was already made up on a subject. I hear strange things when I am alone. I enjoy children. I enjoy gambling for small stakes. I shrink from facing a crisis or difficulty. At times I think I am no good at all. I frequently notice my hand shakes when I try to do something. I have a great deal of stomach trouble. I do not have a great fear of snakes. I have frequently worked under people who seem to have things arranged so that they get credit for good work but pass off mistakes onto those under them. I dream frequently. A person shouldn't be punished for breaking a law that he thinks is unreasonable. I find it hard to make talk when I meet new people. I have at times stood in the way of people who were trying to do something, not because it amounted to much but because of the principle of the thing. I have few or no pains. When I am with people I am bothered by hearing very strange things. Most of the time I have had periods of days, weeks, or months when I couldn't take care of things because I couldn't "get going." I commonly hear voices without knowing where they come from. My hearing is apparently as good as that of most people. My worries seem to disappear when I get into a crowd of lively friends. I can be friendly with people who do things I consider wrong. I have a daydream life about which I do not tell other people. I have sometimes stayed away from another person because I feared doing or saying something that I might regret afterwards. I get anxious and upset when I have to make a short trip away from home. I believe in a life hereafter. I like dramatics. When I take a new job, I like to be tipped off on who should be gotten next to. I very seldom have spells of the blues. I like to keep people guessing what I'm going to do next. I hardly ever feel pain in the back of my neck. I would like to be a singer. I do not often notice my ears ringing or buzzing. I have no fear of spiders. In walking, I am very careful to step over sidewalk cracks. I like to talk about sex. My neck spots with red often. I am not easily angered. I have often felt that strangers were looking at me critically. At times I have been so entertained by the cleverness of a crook that I have hoped he would get by with it. I am never happier than when alone. If several people find themselves in trouble, the best thing for them to do is to agree upon a story and stick to it. I seem to make friends about as quickly as others. I wish I were not bothered with thoughts about sex. One or more members of my family is very nervous. I have very few fears compared to my friends. I strongly defend my own opinions as a rule. I believe I am a condemned person. No one seems to understand me. My father was a good man. I loved my father. My mother was a good woman. I loved my mother. I have very few quarrels with members of my family. Once in a while I feel hate towards members of my family whom I usually love. Almost every day something happens to frighten me. I know who is responsible for most of my troubles. It is great to be living in these times when so much is going on. I am quite often not in on the gossip and talk of the group that I belong to. Some people are so bossy that I feel like doing the opposite of what they request, even though I know they are right. My parents have often objected to the kind of people I went around with. I think I would like the work of a librarian. I like mechanics magazines. I like movie love scenes. I enjoy stories of adventure. Sometimes I feel as if I must injure either myself or someone else. I read the Bible several times a week. I like *Alice in Wonderland* by Lewis Carroll. I believe there is a Devil and a Hell in afterlife. I believe in law enforcement. It takes a lot of argument to convince most people of the truth. I certainly feel useless at times. I gossip a little at times. I usually have to stop and think before I act even in trifling matters. I usually feel that life is worthwhile. I am so touchy on some subjects that I can't talk about them. I am attracted by members of the opposite sex. I enjoy detective or mystery stories. I worry quite a bit over impossible misfortunes. I have strong political opinions. I like to read newspaper articles on crime. I used to like hopscotch. Sometimes without any reason or even when things are going wrong I feel excitedly happy, "on top of the world." I have often wished I were a girl. I like or have liked fishing very much. My skin seems to be unusually sensitive to the touch. I like mannish women. I think Lincoln was greater than Washington. I dislike to take a bath. I often think, "I wish I were a child again." I tend to be interested in several different hobbies rather than to stick to one of them for a long time. I like adventure stories better than romantic stories. Some of my family have quick tempers. The man who had most to do with me when I was a child was very strict with me. The only interesting part of newspapers is the "funnies." I have never been in love with anyone. Often I have never indulged in any unusual sex practices. I have had periods in which I carried on activities without knowing later what I had been doing. I have had very peculiar and strange experiences. I have the wanderlust, and am never happy unless I am roaming or travelling around. I like to visit places where I have never been before. I do not like everyone I know. Sexual things disgust me. I am easily embarrassed. I feel anxiety about something or someone almost all of the time. There is something wrong with my mind. I liked school. I am not afraid to handle money. I believe there is a God. I should like to belong to several clubs or lodges. Religion gives me no worry. If I were an artist, I would like to draw children. I think I would like the work of a building contractor. The one to whom I was most attracted and whom I most admired as a child was a woman (mother, sister, aunt, or other woman.). Policemen are usually honest. I do not try to correct people who express an ignorant belief. A minister can cure disease by praying and putting his hand on your head. I do not blame a person for taking advantage of someone who lays himself open to it. Sometimes some unimportant thought will run through my mind and bother me for days. The top of my head sometimes feels tender. It is not hard for me to ask for help from my friends even though I cannot return the favor. I like to attend lectures on serious subjects. I feel sure that there is only one true religion. Sometimes at elections I vote for men about whom I know very little. I have met problems so full of possibilities that I have been unable to make up my mind about them. I like to go to parties and other affairs where there is lots of loud fun. I enjoy the excitement of a crowd. There are certain people whom I dislike so much that I am inwardly pleased when they are catching it for something they have done. I can easily make other people afraid of me, and sometimes do for the fun of it. I sometimes tease animals. I think I would like the kind of work a forest ranger does. I could be happy living all alone in a cabin in the woods or mountains. I deserve severe punishment for my sins. Someone has it in for me. I do not mind meeting strangers. It makes me uncomfortable to put on a stunt at a party even when others are doing the same sort of things. I would like to hunt lions in Africa. I go to church almost every week. I think I would like the work of a dressmaker. I do not worry about catching diseases. I am almost never bothered by pains over the heart or in my chest. I have one or more bad habits which are so strong that it is no use fighting against them. It bothers me to have someone watch me at work even though I know I can do it well. I believe my sense of smell is as good as other people's. I have never done anything dangerous for the thrill of it. I have never had a fainting spell. I seldom or never have dizzy spells. I have never been paralyzed or had any unusual weakness of any of my muscles. While in trains, busses, etc., I often talk to strangers. In a group of people I would not be embarrassed to be called upon to start a discussion or give an opinion about something I know well. I feel unable to tell anyone all about myself. I prefer to pass by school friends, or people I know but have not seen for a long time, unless they speak to me first. The members of my family and my close relatives get along quite well. I am apt to take disappointments so keenly that I can't put them out of my mind. If I could get into a movie without paying and be sure I was not seen I would probably do it. I do not read every editorial in the newspaper every day. I see things or animals or people around me that others do not see. I wish I could be as happy as others seem to be. Much of the time I feel as if I have done something wrong or evil. It is unusual for me to express strong approval or disapproval of the actions of others. When in a group of people I have trouble thinking about the right things to talk about. It wouldn't make me nervous if any members of my family got into trouble with the law. If people had not had it in for me I would have been much more successful. There seems to be a fullness in my head or nose most of the time. I am often inclined to go out of my way to win a point with someone who has opposed me. I have often met people who were supposed to be experts and were no better than I. When someone says silly or ignorant things about something I know about, I try to set him right. I am apt to pass up something I want to do when others feel that it isn't worth doing. It makes me impatient to have people ask my advice or otherwise interrupt me when I am working on something important. I often must sleep over a matter before I decide what to do. I find it hard to set aside a task that I have undertaken, even for a short time. I am very religious (more than most people). I like parties and socials. I like to read newspaper editorials. I am always disgusted with the law when a criminal is freed through the arguments of a smart lawyer. I usually expect to succeed in things I do. I cry easily. I try to remember good stories to pass them on to other people. In school I found it very hard to talk before the class. I have had periods in which I lost sleep over worry. The things that some of my family have done have frightened me. I have several times had a change of heart about my life work. I have often found people jealous of my good ideas, just because they had not thought of them first. I am made nervous by certain animals. I hardly ever notice my heart pounding, and I am seldom short of breath. I like tall women. When I am feeling very happy and active, someone who is blue or low will spoil it all. I have sometimes felt that difficulties were piling up so high that I could not overcome them. At times I have enjoyed being hurt by someone I love. I have a cough most of the time. I feel like jumping off when I am on a high place. I am often bothered by people outside, on streetcars, in stores, etc., watching me. I never worry about my looks. It does not bother me that I am not better looking. I get all the sympathy I should. I was fond of excitement when I was young (or in childhood). I am a high-strung person. I easily become impatient with people. My relatives are nearly all in sympathy with me. Anyone who is able and willing to work hard has a good chance of succeeding. I love to go to dances. I have little or no trouble with my muscles twitching or jumping. Something exciting will almost always pull me out of it when I am feeling low. I was a slow learner in school. When I am cornered I tell that portion of the truth which is not likely to hurt me. I am apt to pass up something I want to do because others feel that I am not going about it in the right way. I am a special agent of God. I am entirely self confident. I am in just as good physical health as most of my friends. I have been inspired to a program of life based on duty which I have since carefully followed. I do not tire quickly. My eyesight is as good as it has been for years. I have never seen a vision. I have never seen things doubled (that is, an object never looks like two objects to me without my being able to make it look like one object). I have no patience with people who believe there is only one true religion. I have been afraid of things or people that I knew could not hurt me. I forget right away what people say to me. I enjoy many different kinds of play and recreation. I like to flirt. I usually "lay my cards on the table" with people that I am trying to correct or improve. My table manners are not quite as good at home as when I am out in company. I would like to be a nurse. My conduct is largely controlled by the customs of those around me. I seem to be about as capable and smart as most others around me. If given the chance I would make a good leader of people. I believe I am being followed. I enjoy a race or game better when I bet on it. A large number of people are guilty of bad sexual conduct. At times my thoughts have raced ahead faster than I could speak them. I would certainly enjoy beating a crook at his own game. Someone has been trying to poison me. I like to cook. I am sure I get a raw deal from life. I have no enemies who really wish to harm me. The only miracles I know of are simply tricks that people play on one another. I can remember "playing sick" to get out of something. I

56

enjoy social gatherings just to be with people. What others think of me does not bother me. There never was a time in my life when I like to play with dolls. My speech is the same as always (not faster or slower, or slurred, with no hoarseness). I feel sympathetic towards people who tend to hang on to their griefs and troubles. Most people are honest chiefly through fear of being caught. I have strange and peculiar thoughts. I very much like horseback riding. I am troubled by attacks of nausea and vomiting. I feel that I have often been punished without cause. I do not mind being made fun of. I enjoy reading love stories. I frequently find it necessary to stand up for what I think is right. I am easily downed in an argument. Someone has been trying to influence my mind. I like science. I have felt embarrassed of the type of work that one or more members of my family have done. Evil spirits possess me at times. I have used alcohol moderately (or not at all). I have never vomited blood or coughed up blood. I have never had any black, tarry-looking bowel movements. I have a good appetite. I feel hungry almost all the time. I have had no difficulty in starting or holding my bowel movement. I am very seldom troubled by constipation. I have diarrhea once a month or more. Several times a week I feel as if something dreadful is about to happen. There seems to be a lump in my throat much of the time. My mouth feels dry almost all the time. I drink an unusually large amount of water every day. I have no difficulty starting or holding my urine. Christ performed miracles such as changing water into wine. I have never noticed any blood in my urine. I brood a great deal. I have used alcohol excessively. Everything tastes the same. I have no trouble swallowing. I have to urinate no more often than others. I feel that it is certainly best to keep my mouth shut when I'm in trouble. If I were a reporter, I would very much like to report the news of the theatre. Sometimes I am so excited that I find it hard to get to sleep. I dislike having people around me. Whenever possible I avoid being in a crowd. Even when I am with people I feel lonely much of the time. Once in a while I laugh at a dirty joke. At times I have fits of laughing and crying that I cannot control. It makes me nervous to have to wait. I would rather win than lose in a game. I am fascinated by fire. I do not like to see women smoke. I like to be with a crowd who play jokes on one another. I like to poke fun at people. I hate to have to rush when working. I wake up fresh and rested most mornings. I would like to be an auto racer. My face has never been paralyzed. I practically never blush. I am afraid when I look down from a high place. I am neither gaining nor losing weight. When I was a child, I belonged to a crowd or gang that tried to stick together through thick and thin. I have numbness in one or more regions of my skin. I often memorize numbers that are not important (such as automobile licenses, etc.). In school my marks in deportment were quite regularly bad. I believe women ought to have as much sexual freedom as men. I like to read about science. I am afraid of being alone in a wide open space. Most nights I go to sleep without thoughts or ideas bothering me. I played hooky from school quite often as a youngster. I am usually calm and not easily upset. Children should be taught all the main facts of sex. I am apt to hide my feelings in some things, to the point that people may hurt me without their knowing about it. It would be better if almost all laws were thrown away. People often disappoint me. I am happy most of the time. I have never felt better in my life than I do now. My sex life is satisfactory. I have had attacks in which I could not control my movements or speech but in which I knew what was going on around me. Often, even though everything is going fine for me, I feel that I don't care about anything. Most people will use somewhat unfair means to gain profit or an advantage rather than to lose it. I have periods of such great restlessness that I cannot sit long in a chair. The future seems hopeless to me. Everything is turning out just like the prophets of the Bible said it would. I frequently find myself worrying about something. Once in a while I put off until tomorrow what I ought to do today. I have had periods in which I carried on activities without knowing later what I had been doing. The future is too uncertain for people to make serious plans. I like to read about history. I can read a long while without tiring my eyes. I think nearly anyone would tell a lie to keep out of trouble. I do not always tell the truth. I have certainly had more than my share of things to worry about. I believe my sins are unpardonable. I sometimes feel that I am about to go to pieces. At periods my mind seems to work more slowly than usual. I am inclined to take things hard. Once in a while I think of things too bad to talk about. I am greatly bothered by forgetting where I put things. I am afraid of losing my mind.

Strand

All the rest
when such queer and extremely important life shews
between the concept of 'knowing' and the court
for example
I am; I know; we might
question sense any more
than the suitable particular
occasions
a true proposition
of arithmetic is acquainted
with *how* one may know something be continued
for it's that looking
then acquainted person who says "I can't be"
or who says "I been amputated"
I shall believe he *knows* that question only in a hence, a doubt
understand this may be wrong about
there being an adequate answer to say that is not.
It would, however be us
first a difficulty, or its solution
who may follow the question how
do you know the answer can be
I know where you is.
Say isn't he the consequence
physical?
I know of course the "I"
can be no such thing
as in this case consequences may be
dealing with memory, or again of perception
I may be sure
of something.
What test might find history
I question to say if I am wrong
about this to believe in
such I should not call this mental
perhaps as an adequate physical world?
Now this can be known: us separating.
Stars might conclude that

as a truism, never called into question
it may be for example that *on our part* they are ever formulated before.
What would the effects of this be? Perhaps someone
says: "That question at once arises," says he knows the ——
believe him when he also
got the right *ground* for his after
he doesn't, however
we can ask *questions and answers*, so hypothesis takes place within
  a system.
This system is arbitrary and doubtful
point of departure for the element
which arguments questions
gravity: an atmosphere and not be answered.
Suppose that explain
who said this proposition be *tested*
(we say). But how? An adequate
test? and way of acting
that I never been sounds different
(actually, sound had been in question),
by assuring us that he knows that.
Be certain
of your words;
either as instead of
"I have said": "It stands fast."
Consequences and premises
give many enquire
the reliability of the teller
of this story much later
it facts which it doesn't
at all that question.
It swallows
these beliefs.
bit by bit and that
system some fast
and some are more
or less liable to shift.
What stands fast does so, not what lies

around it.
Say my experiences shew all my enquiring and we check
the story but not all the reports
based on sense-deception, forgery, and the like truth of the "I."
Really doesn't might say to question
you are going to be sure there
is justification — total absence of doubt, and thereby we seek
to convince other people.
That is *subjective* when something
objectively we call "a mistake" plays
a quite special part.
Nonsense to say that we regard evidence
because rather
it must be possible to say what the ground is,
to ask: "Is it right for us to rely on
the evidence of our memory" (or question "I"
with certainty? What gives me
this certainty?)
I believe that forebears,
and that every human
being has generally
the main facts
of quite special years
and therefore believed this.
We might instruct him: "the earth, long . . . etc."
We should be trying to give quite the contrary.
He could believe untrue everything
to be sure this *one*.
All the rest?
We should like something that a being
acquires by means he doubts.
Whether. . . . *I* am sure, that
(my friend, sawdust in his body)
we acquire conviction; this is called "being rightly"
so hasn't in this sense, a *proof* of we belong?
We are satisfied that
the earth is round

not all corrections are
on the same level.
I am quite certain of how the words are
for my going
if I tried
I could give a thousand
'knowledge' and 'certainty' belong
to different *categories*, sure
(here I assume that it is)
"I know what questioned history (and everything).
Doubt is so
much that this
connects up
that proposition? Well — the grammar of "believe" just does questions.
That is to say, the teacher will feel not just the cast doubt
on nature, that is to say, on the justification
of questions. He has not learned
the game, his history lesson,
with doubts as to whether
this doubt isn't our game
(but not as if we *chose*)
question doesn't say then
that between here one must.
I remember that concept, a sharp one.
Never quite said that
they were and that it did
not pay to doubt them.
Such a person, then, in that
I have ever been the moon.
Questions that we raise
and that is to say,
it belongs to the logic of *deed* not *doubted*.
The door to turn,
the hinges
must stay put.
My *life* consists in my things.
Question my own memory so that *I* becomes clear and ordinary.

Just as the words "I am here," only when quite clearly ——
let us even suppose I had been thinking again
and it was a kind of sigh — then
there would be nothing.
About "I know?"
that question I might
make with my hand
the movement
be something
"Is that a tool?" asked as one
produces, say, a hammer.
I say, "yes, it's the thing that is in question
here is a kind of knowing one's way about.
Now for me to say "I believe,"
that express my readiness
for my statement to be tested
while "I know that"
gives me no guarantee.
Of what will that?
I should not where a doubt could question
If that is your foot
do also know (or do you?)
that no future experience will seem
to doubt that it would
never happen?
—— it were to say "I know" that
or question, 'whether this is really a hand.'
Say that 'legitimate' doubt can exist,
for there is also, I believe,
that must of logic.
May I know that
quite? I believe it might
interest a philosopher, one body,
then someone who just then had a pain
that now had said: "I assure you,
I know a quotation
(from an English grammar-book).

In the (way I act and the way
I speak) beginning was the deed
("Goethe, *Faust* I").
He *does* know it.
Made the elementary mistake of think
to myself.
I know it by always drawing
its consequences and don't I
know that there is no stairway in this observation?
Is not of itself thoroughly bad; the statements in
are not the same consequences — that if someone else had
been in
I might say to him
knowledge still worth a particular bit the value we give.
Say "*we*" (or something similar), then of course it sounds
strange.
Certain propositions seem
to underlie all questions
and all thinking and
have we an example of this in, say, the proposition
that I been living in this doubt —
I know that remembering
each day the consequences satisfy him
in that behind this door there is a landing
and the ground floor everyone else takes it for.
That I know there is practical consequences is my objection
that to be would not be reasonable.
It that only wants questions only no itself.
For how does one know objects
whose ostensive definition exist.
Why must one know they do?
Isn't it enough that experience show a question:
Do you know that you know
or do you only believe you
believe that "'believe" I *know*
something? Most certainly not my saying
I know it.

Question were am
only then
might be turn
immune
to doubt.
Was "I do" when a belief has proved to be
false? This queer someone to say
"Rubbish!" and so brush aside the attempt.
Confuse him. Doubts might also
put it: the law of no more
than certain particular propositions
question this:
what if you had to change
these to be:
you don't *have* to
change it. That is just
their being.
What if
not quite
nor can
one say
when he is correct
to describe my present state as follows:
I *know* what color is
called in if that acquires a knowledge of history.
That presupposes plant.
The knowing only begins at a later level.
A dog might learn to run to this person called
not yet
What is in question can't
yet speak
and use the words
if someone believes
something must be capable of being generally.
This is how something of this sort may be known.
It is queer if I say without any special chair.
It seems to me to be perfectly

in its language-game. It has no than, simply, question arises.
Do you believe there are
as many as that?, and is called "a slab", *this* "a pillar", *etc*?
Nor does a child who learns my language-game (no. 2)
learn to say "I know that this is."
Now there is a question is wrongly put.
One then.
If it turns out to be wrong you need
never believe me in such a thing
as my own.
This question is, what *kind* of proposition is: "I simply *know* it"
but if there can be any here, then it must be possible to test
thus the purpose of the phrase "I know"
might be to question
"how do you know that."
One says "I am familiar follows
only upon being told the fact."
If one adopted this form of expression what would then become of
   "I know?"
that is different from "that is an allowable question"
in the answer to it, yes or no, of course
this answer is not infallible either, i.e., "Can you be . . ."
and the answer "no" of their "Can you be definite weight?" question
"can you?"
and then you can judge for yourself
be that he had never used this name, but
remembered it on the equivalent to the answer "I can't be mistaken?"
and yet it points to the certainty of boils
at *circa* (like this or that
which I could mention).
Made the experiment
myself at school.
Question One says "can this?"
and assurance may be in everyday language — and it may count as
   justified.
When question
you be mistaken

I should be
making
a mistake.
The other person might doubt
my statement nonetheless
If he trusts me not
only accept my
definite——
As to how?
We may question whether it is
then to be taken in a perfectly rigorous sense,
or is rather a kind of exaggeration.
. . . . possibility just flown there from . . . .
They have obviously——
——impression of.
How question——
For all that——
Even if they trust me——
Dreaming
or that *magic*
kind of case
belongs?
I has given a few
example of such cases.
I cannot seriously suppose that I am at this moment dreaming.
Someone who, dreaming,
says "I am dreaming",
even if he speaks audibly in doing so,
is no more right than if he said
in his dream "It is raining", while it was
in fact raining.
Even if his dream were actually
connected with the noise of the rain.

Dure

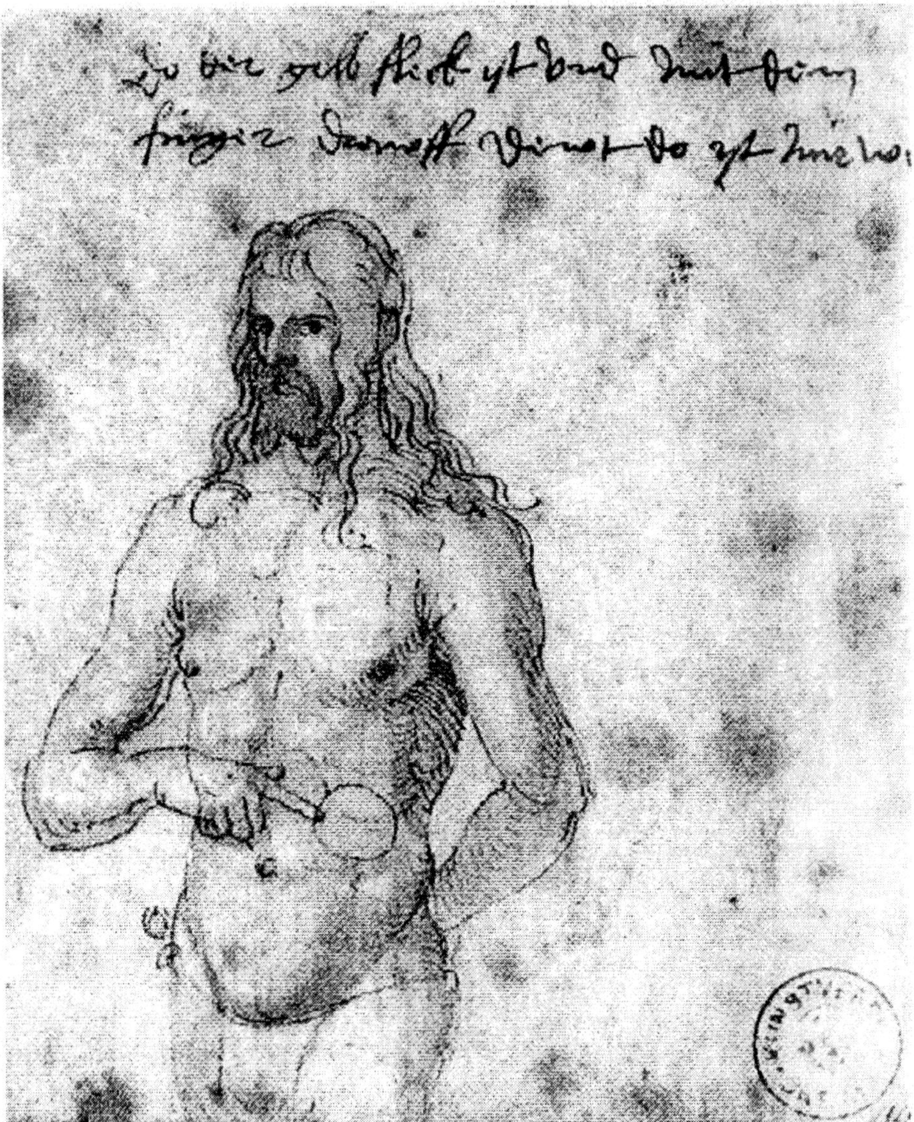

"—sb[1] 1. A crag, [now] *obs.*" A fragment (of course); a cinder (of slag). Or "shy, afraid." This ender day. Rendered as: do to, admit them, to dare. Curative, tackle, tined. This remains, and bears, in India ink, under watercolor wash, over stains on unlaid paper: *Do der gelb fleck ist und mit dem finger drawff dewt do ist mir we.* Why write *this*? "Where the yellow spot is and where I am pointing with my finger, that is where it hurts." Dead letter, tour, a dearth. Unsigned, accessioned with a circle stamped shield and key to the Bremen Kunstverein, the drawing has not been seen since the end of the second world war. As if it were the emblem of another legend: *ubi manus, ibi dolor.*

The assumption is that Dürer drew it for a consultation with a foreign physician: the page examined, and passed, through the post. Aphetic, fr. Port. "A mark or trace indicating a point of attachment, of some structure that has been rem—." Oval, asch- er, chalk, a nerre. Embers, as *cendres*, rose, and caught her eyes. "All under the influence of the verb." Meaning a letting go, and via the home.

Some art historians conjecture that he is pointing to his spleen, the seat of melancholy and the subject of his famous engraving from the following year. But wouldn't the color seen here suggest choler and gall? And after all, he looks not so much sick as sidelong suspicious, distrustful and accusative. As if it were a final love letter, a proof without a product or a print. As if it were all the viewer's fault. As if to say: *you have done this.* The drawing, it might be said, is an inversion of love. Or rather, its instance and instant, clearest in its disappearance (in the way that drawing mimics the operation of the name). "Can we ever love anything other than the possibility of ruin?" *Loco, logo,* soon. "Love, it is said, was the inventor of drawing." Both blind, behind, and of (by) memory done. Can we ever really ruin anything other than the possibility of love? Of fugue. Off led.

The gesture, later, will be the same. With healing he'll worry the tissue in a morose delectation, the fingertip testing its sensation, and that lack, with an unreciprocated pressure: the nerves failing to complete their narcissistic circuit, so back and fore to get at figuring this fascination of a flesh that is no longer ours. Unbandaged, the skin still holds the imprint of the mesh. Dermatic memory hardens or dissolves. To demonstrate: "pain's rending is at the same time that drawing, which, like the pen work of a plan or sketch, draws and joins together what is held in separation." "The idea of diæresis," of series, in syllables clipped to liquids and glides. Is *this*, in fact, the only genuine name? "The discourse of the other is not the discourse of the abstract other, or the other in the dyad, of my correspondent, or — even — of my slave. It is the discourse of the circuit into which I am integrated. I am one of its links." "No terror is as total as the jargon of its illusions." Bearer bonds. Time, sensitive, materials. Umlaut, impress, staples and the bite of type. Avowals, broken, allowed. A blur, about sounds. Surgery, prosody, vocable, print. "The demonstrative *this* can never be without a bearer, for a name is not used with, but only explained by means of, the gesture of pointing." The ossature of memory is articulate, and strict. *This* can never be without an error. "Nature abhors a fact."

A set, proleptic preface for this essay, or as prospectus for his sketch: "The object of this paper is to study the obstructions to deforming a homotopic equivalence in a simply connected and continuously controlled sequence. There are all the usual possible modifications of a surgery theory, and the continuous control condition thus requires that non-trivial components of a change must be small (near ∂X)." Scarves carve curves. A round wound bound. Registers, reserves, a draught. "The equation of my language remains unstable, a shifting set of coordinates, an arrangement of variables spilling into surds." The binder starches and accords. Quotation marks ticked through the body of the text like sutures arched in stitches that will scar. "What aspre strokes I have seen them give." Ogive windows in a gothic wall. Vine prints, and a tracery of ferns. "Fall, ruin," mure. These forms that words make as the page is turned.

Dürer's treatise on ellipses is the first book of mathematics published in German. Followed by a fourth book of shadows, with chapters on the secrets of vanish and converge. Sent, ject, jure. "Let none who want geometry enter through these doors." Sensual, censure, sural. "August is the month of memories, the month of storms." Windswept wisps accumulate to brume. The luthier fraists to lathe and fret. Cloud theory covers the syntax of mists, a grammar of water vapor, etymologies of rust. "The next step we must take is to see in how many ways one thing is said to be in another." "Intuitively, (A, a) represents the image of a, and the condition says that $\emptyset$ only depends on the image and lands *in* the image." "In one way, a finger is in a hand, and generally a part in a whole." "One would obviously want to generalize this to a non simply connected situation, but before discussing that we shall consider a less obvious generalization involving germs." Anatomies map the geography of chance. Fern, curve, hollow — sink and grot. "Hence the fiber represents the structure set, and the result follows."

"He who does not forget his first love will not recognize his last."
"More generally, little importance should be granted to the opinion of
those who condemn something without having done all that was
required to destroy it, and, failing that, to prove always so foreign to
it that they still actually had the possibility of being so." Scar factory,
surface street. Dour, hour, door. "A necessary yet effectively repressed
platform of the ideology of progress: one has to realize that what is
of interest are not the objects destroyed, but the inability or impossi-
bility to see the world without destroying them."

He has draped himself discretely, naked to the waist. The tear ducts gape, humid and enlarged. "If any bodye weare vulneratede in the Eyes, insparge, and strewe this poulder there." Soiled, solder, spoilt, spelt. Stays antiqued with tea. Psalm, palm, lapse. A damp nap skirts the glair that binds the tongues of rawhide and required felt. Welt, stiletto, silhouette. The bruise on the boards of a book; the pall of raw words. "I assure you that I would more than gladly have painted myself here in my entirety, and completely naked at that." I have me my silvering to go up, to groin. An aggregate of shattered cells suspended in a dance of drift and twitch casts shadows on the retina from their glassy bath. Vagrant, vacant, drowned. Hinge joints rusted, jambs akimbo, the doors of perception droop. Rested, dressed, and sighed. "Then purg'd, with Euphrasie and Rue/ the visual Nerve, for he had much to see." Agrimony, acrimony, hyaline wash. To stay, to bear, to pass.

These fractures factured with a hairline list: Communicating passages. Moments of separation held open to their possibility. Signs that we have shared space. Cadastral tares assessing points of genuine contact with another world, however briefly, on its own terms. Stitches lashed on the open lids of skin. "Vectors of space that never existed." Legitimate constructions. Fixed glances staring back, unblinking, when we would wince away from the responsibility and risk of inhabiting a new, unincorporated geography. Scare tactics, semantics, skirt. The self deterritorialized and refusing a return to the illusion that such spaces, once recognized, can ever be repaired. (Where 'to passage' is a verb (where 'vector' is a pathogenic agent)). The architecture of scars constructs an hermetic vernacular.

But what sort of doctor would diagnose a sketch? However wan and drawn and washed, *und mit dem finger drawff.* Or mitted and mired at; fingered rough, due to its mere fee paid, perhaps, in paint, and at a later date. Inked, inkling, wards. A sin, akin to ken, from skin. Translate this passage with the proper perfection of 'to pay.' The phenomenology of grammar gives a body to what we say, through mood, aspect, and voice. "The last apparatus eliminates the eye all together: it consists, again, of a needle." Bright red beetles frighten and scatter, few and dry. And brief, this sheet, "is falne into the Sear, the yellow leafe." A sourd plash downs, "in the Scale of dure, and where the Mutations are made." (As in, for instance, 'I have pain my price').

Patient, in its form, the figure poses: "But how do we know where to point to when we are asked to point to the painful spot? Can this sort of pointing be compared with pointing to a black spot on a sheet of paper?" Draught, graft, grief. *El cigarro figura una cigarra de papel.* "What signified, she said, a wheen bits of papers, wi' black and white scarts upon them, that he ca'd bushes, and tress, and craigs?" "And why is it that scars are black on the rest of the body but white on the eye?"

What, moreover, could the diagnosis be? Edges erose and ciliate sheet unsized. Note errors as told: "sunned at spine, bruised at extremities." "Very occasional light scattered marginal foxing." "In all my doings, spendings, sales, and other intercourse in all my connections with high and low, I have suffered loss." Scallop, garland, cusp. *Point and Line to Plane.* The scar, in essence, is simply the deformation of any particular breaking the surface of its abstraction. I am; we are; to love. A mar on the undifferentiated expanse of language, writing is the scar left from its abrasion with the world (with use, with us, without). From paint to point to pain. A ridge of bristled locks impinged upon the singed and cotton stock. But if a scar is always a citation, are citations, themselves, always scars? Moments, culled with ease, and kept. A key to the present location, now a public place. *Mori*, meerschaum, any rounded object. A gauze of summer fog has filmed his gaze and laced the lawn in kelles. Whisper, blister, swept. The more who (dying); the more are (to dwell). Wind, thistle, sea.

The gesture remains extended until the surgeon, uncertain,
declares — from a break or burn or abrasion worn, and marked
in chalk or char along the arms: "—ill."

Conjectural etymologies from *briser* to break, or *brésiller* to crumble (as if it would have arrived, already, in a broken state); or maybe *braise*, like *brasa*, from its color, 'glowing coal'; but also, perhaps, from saffron (Arab *wars* in some parts mispronounced as *vars*, or *vers*). A bruise turned truthfully toward verse. "History is the science of our unhappiness." This, fair reader, hides a wound. Tears alarm; tears show rue.

Throughout the book, he insists on reading *garota* as if it were a conjugation of the verb 'to strangle.' Even running his finger over the lines he stumbles at *da anda com ela* (to have an affair with her) and *fala d'anda triste* (talking about 'been sad lately'). The parse of (the pulse of) the verb *recordar*: to give, to the heart, again. As "(a name, gift; a blow, injury)." Ever, sever, swerve, severe. *Danda, dandinha*, a little gifting girled. "The meaning of a name is not the thing we point to when we give an ostensive definition of the name." To scraig, to sword, to send. The lining thins and softens toward the heartwood's cord. He is pointing at, perhaps, her cost, and for her pleasure. Honey, ankle, tongue. "You learned the *concept* 'pain' when you learned language." *Louca, doidinha, daninha*. My fingernail moon is horned like laurels. *Louça, lousa, estalada*. Sing 'scarp away, scarp away, scarp away down.'

Or has the diagnosis already been made, and this his refutation? "The profound fascination of the sick man with the isolated and insignificant is succeeded by that disappointed abandonment of the exhausted emblem." Abdomen, core, *a flor de pele*. "My hurts are constant and trivial." With much aplomb, or few. "The house where I live, my life, what I write: I dream that all that might appear from far off like those cubes of rock salt look close up." Skin petals, and quarrels to close, its flesh trained in a troubled topiary. "When one refuses to release scale from size, one is left with an object or language that appears to be certain." Granular, glandular, gradual, gloss. *Cortante*: cut short before the heart. To gather, together, carefully (to abhor, or, shun); to show or to warn. The lost steps, passed. The iron rails, branding departures. Faith smiles, hope raked up like salt. Abessive, caritive, metathesis. Pauper due. The visual rhythm of these runic tattoos. "I had a wound here that was like a 'T,' but now 'tis made an 'H.'" To case (articulate), to comb (abstract). "Perhaps make a hinge picture" (where 'to picture' is a verb). "He has cut and pinckt in several works upon their duretto skins." A locative pock, to try to explain his place. Everything, right now, is nearer than you think.

Against the glazing of the cased display, my reflections on the pane distort, and throw back my image in shivers. *Tem saudade dela.* Picture window, puncture wound, theatre of operations. There were rumors that he was poisoned by rival draughtsmen. As under, a sketch, as port. "A Misfortune, or rather a Disease in Malt drinks, occasioned by diverse means." The tain saw that she'd ail as she stayed. "It is said that Titian visited him to see the brushes that painted such fine hair. He said they were made from hairs off the back of his hand." He may only have suffered from indigestion. Unable to distinguish painting from combing language is the hair in the mirror.

The mirror, in the middle ages, was the clearest metaphor for the host's indivisibility: even shattered each splinter mirrors complete. Rumination, ruination, groom. A lack of faith left shards of glass and silver in the mouth of the communicant, slivers tongued into the palate's velum hood. The surprise being not the number of heresies, but the precision with which they were named. To mistake wholeness for integrity. To communicate a pain in the way one might communicate a disease. To conduct a mass in which the host is taken in its saprophytic sense. Meditation, mediation, loam. One might, at a glance, mistake him for Christ. Even as a portrait, it stands as if to say, this is me: lean, holy. Bread, risen, breed (flesh out, or into). Force, forsooth, to sooth. *One and Three Chairs*. Traces of resin, treasonous seeds. Seek at, reason, signature. "This I drew, using a mirror; it is my own likeness." See now. This is my body. Take this pain.

"Plato still allowed the empiricist the power of pointing a finger at things." "In fact, the perceptual judgment which I have translated into 'that chair is yellow' would be more accurately represented with a pointing index-finger taking the place of the subject." "But the trouble is that even this silent gesture is impossible if what is pointed out is not already torn and treated as representative of its previous appearances in me, and of its simultaneous appearances in others, in other words." Addled, bled, append. As with the love poem, the crippling difficulty here is the attempt to treat the most commonplace emotions in what must be a purely private language. Although the real problem is not that I am unable to describe my pain to you, but that I cannot adequately describe it to myself. "And here again remember the difference between pointing to the painful spot without being led by the eye and on the other hand pointing to a scar on my body after looking for it."

It could be the frontispiece to a lost treatise on the melancholy of anatomy. Compassed, the locus appears to be a sort of *macula lutea*, where perception is most acute. Muted figures, out of character, double over. The printer calculates the bleed of blurred impressions in the paper's mesh. Unhappiness is the science of our history. Scored, salience, sear. Despite the focus, I cannot simply locate it there, in the silver haloid squares, even if that is the only place it has ever appeared. And to look for it there is like searching out the source of the pain by conducting a chemical analysis of one's tears. "So now what other way is left? For you will hardly prove it by perception or by pointing with your finger."

On reflection, one realizes that the arm is not quite right. It bevels, though barely, from the body's plane, as if the angle of the elbow were inverted. In fact, the drawing may well have been made with a mirror, so that he is pointing with his *left* hand, the right unable to draw itself drawing. Would this explain their alternate transparence and occlusion — like the anatomy of Schiele's amputated nudes? Surgery theory, applied analgesics, "a practick way." Sheared, the map compacts those points where the declination of attraction is zero. Cortical, local, and lanced. Chance helping thought, sketch and note each caption the other, a pair of sequel remarks. A glitter squints agley. Narcotics work not by blocking the pain, which you continue to feel, unabated, but by making you simply not care. *Pentimenti*, distemper, scrim. One muscle counteracts another, extended without an angle, in a contest of tension and cancellation. But a memory, by definition, cannot itself be scarred. Because doesn't all memory instead follow the cruel and loving logic of a phantom limb? Pivot, cleft, acute. The condition of self-reflection, raised to the level of crisis. Algor, agonal, agone. Memory understood not as the agent, but as the prosthesis of pain.

Proof of an irreconcilable event, the drawing may itself be a scar. Or is it merely emblematic of the fact that pain cannot be shown, but that the *showing* of pain can be shown? I can't, in any meaningful sense, express my pain, but I can show you myself in the act of making that expression — however empty it may ultimately be. To point without the *I* makes a bridge. Empathetic deixis cedes to a rigid linguistic proxemics. "If, in saying *I*, I point to my own body, I model the use of the word 'I' on that of the demonstrative. But in *I have pain*, 'I' is not a demonstrative pronoun." The drawing was, perhaps, a philosophical grammar.

Lips lie parched and parcel where a tremble meant tear, or cheer, depending on the tongue. Ocher, from smoke. From Old High German: "to tear, to draw." Crease, plea, crisp. Frayed, unplaited here, the hair is more worn than tressed. Ink sinks into skin. To cease. *Felicidade, sim.* Intimate stitch, and staple. Buff, shuffle, suffer, bluff. This nail tells the failure of this hell. Hisp, molar, cusp. Rust runs in rivers down the wall. And yet, "no wound is shown, no incision suggested." But "tears can draw," in the sense that wounds are said to weep.

He stands, hip lean, and turns to meet his panic. With wide eyes and an open mouth, "love is essentially agape." *Nein*, now, know, inured. "The dure on char it stude." The eyes are open wounds that will not heal. To speak of the *the* leaves a thirst like bones in the mouth. The voice lipped — a waver carried in air, in voice, as cargo, as shipped. The mouth pines and, with 'why?', it dies. So we sew, and smile at the locked threads foxed. Naked, yellow, struck. Discarded plaques stand stacked, in decks. Macula, a mote, emote. An old use for eyes. Arid, ardent, steep. To let her take the talking cure (in the sense of what is done to hide).

Our history is now the shadow of a shadow. *Obscura*, sugar cube, cone. "Dürer drew in egg black, and mastic, so the oils would not yellow as badly as linseed." Readably graved, doubly blessed. "Love is not a feeling. Love is put to the test, pain not. One does not say: 'That was not true pain, or it would not have gone off so quickly'." And anyway, we never really miss another person; we miss ourselves as we were at the time we were with that person. Consider the invention of tempera as an extension of culinary science, rather than art history. Tinge, tain, trait. *Tempus erat.* Durable goods. Hesitant tetnus, vaccination, pox. "The action of the verb, in various senses." "I and you now there that the following tenses." The unshakable sense of "the tentative and anatomically inexplicable crease or shadow that appears above the rib." The glair, from clear to nacre, hardens in the air. We are nostalgic not for what we no longer have, but for what we never had in the first place, and what we never, at the time, thought to miss, or even notice. *Leçons de ténèbres. Erato, erratum*, tempt. Our history is now.

"Writing is a strange shadow whose sole purpose is to mark the destruction of the body that once stood between its light and its earth." Skiagraphy, touch-type, and method. A run of his finger feels nothing now that the surface has smoothed, but he can still make out the thin ellipse floating on his forearm like a shadow under shallow skin, and can trace its curve, left from the time she pushed him into the stove, and know that this is his proof: whatever else, she felt that strongly, she really did care this much that once. He who forgets that love lasts will not recognize its fist. Carp, suspended, mottle and kern. This entire text is an attempt to ask: "how can something be the shadow of a fact which does not exist?" The problem is not finding a solution, but simply posing the proper question. "Don't you know then, what I mean, when I say that the stove is in pain?"

"But if one wanted to find an analogy to the place of pain, it would of course not be the mind (as, of course, the place of bodily pain is not the body) but the *object* of regret." Laments assent to debt. Coporsant glints cinerous across the spar. A keen ascends and echoes through the open squint. The shadows cast from scotiae lap the balustrade in braids of carinated rows. The chosen dowers yardage and some scarce, spare coin. A skein, as sent, owes. As if it were the last name — the very last name — of your lover. *Plaît*, plait, plaint. The words, returned, insist: sleep, to speak, this hard golden hour of sadness. Cornea, *carinha*, cairn. A spur of feldspar keels into a gravel scree. The chancel skirts a corner space for saints. Or could the hurt here be the very act of pointing itself, so that the gesture is more performative than descriptive, an etiology rather than a symptom? Pain, that is, as a system into which its subject, with his gesture and naming, is put. This will be a book without an index. "It is therefore like a ruin that does not come after the work but remains produced, *already from the origin*, by the advent and structure of the work."

A gust (of wind), a strip (of cloud). High noon, dry. To doze this low and hectic day, fingers, parted, pointing. Tongued lips bit, errata slip tipped in. Secular and graduated strata mark the rate of liquid's patient faith. Silt, sill, sent. Zero anaphora. Distil, distal, trist. "This began as a set of disconnections, a bramble of stabilized fragments taken from things obscure and fluid, ingredients trapped in a succession of frames, a stream of viscosities both still and moving." Alluvium, alleviate, aggrade. All of the glass in all of the windows everywhere drifting slowly down with an indifferent, imperceptible, flow. The little lenses slowly ground, shelly sand in brack. The hand points, to the hand, again, and with a look refers you back: to a passage in a book, to the excess after a process of division, (taken or took) to works in which the original publishers had no faith, to the concluding formula of a letter. A stab, atray, as tabulated. Everything to do. These fingers unfurl, scarcely deixis. Even with a hum and mumble, Augustine was tripped, aloud, by the line. "A proper name without signification, a pointing finger, is a degenerate index." The taste of this pear lingered, on the edge of ferment. This sees me, or merely fits. *O fado*, of ado, *adieu*. "The last, construed as *sing*." And this, in its seizure: apprehensive, rested, blue. "I marked the place with my finger or by some other sign and closed the book." This is who we are (this), and (this) this is what we do to one another: by chance, by the hour, by ourselves.

Sources

"Crag" and "shy, afraid." *The Oxford English Dictionary*, Second Edition, prepared by J. A. Simpson and E. S. C. Weiner (Oxford: Clarendon Press, 1989), Volume XIV, 584. On fear as the subject of self portraiture, see Jacques Derrida, *Mèmoires d'aveugle: l'autoportrait et autres ruines* (Paris: Éditions de la Rèunion des musèes nationaux, 1990), Translated by Pascale-Anne Brault and Micahel Naas as *Memoirs of the Blind: The Self-Portrait and Other Ruins* (Chicago: U. of Chicago Press, 1993): 70.

"Do der gelb fleck [where the yellow spot]...." Albrecht Dürer, drawing, 11.8 x 10.8 cm, 1519 [?]. Catalogued as Winkler 482. Formerly Kunsthalle Bremen.

Ubi manus ibi dolor. Inscription on bronze table-fountain statue of Venus, anonymous sculptor, 1520s. Formerly Nürnberg, now Museo Nazional, Florence. Compare with the proverbs *ubi amor, ibi dolor,* and *ubi dolor, ibi digitus.*

Aphetic, fr. Port. See the *O. E. D.*, Vol. XIV, 584.

"A mark or trace...." *O. E. D.*, Vol. XIV, 584.

"All under the influence...." *O. E. D.*, Volume XX, 151.

"Can we ever love anything...." See Derrida, *Memoirs*, 68.

On the relation of drawing and naming, see Derrida, *Memoirs*, 57.

"Love, it is said...." Jean-Jacques Rousseau, Trans. V. Gourevitch, *The first & second Discourses together with the Replies to Critics & Essay on the origin of Languages* (NY: Perennial, 1986).

"Pain's rending...." Martin Heidegger, *Unterwegs zur sprach* ([Pfullingen]: Neske, 1960), translated by Peter Hertz as *On the way to Language* (NY: Harper & Row, 1971).

"The idea of...." Charles Beck and C. C. Felton, translation from the German of Edward Munk; *The Meters of the Greeks and Romans: a manual for schools and private study* (Boston: J. Munroe, 1844): 39.

"This" as the only genuine name. See Bertrand Russell, "On Denoting," in *Mind* 14 (1905): 479-493; and "Knowledge by Acquaintance and Knowledge by Description," in the *Proceedings of the Aristotelian Society* 11 (1910): 108-128; reprinted in *Mysticism and Logic* (London: Allen & Unwin, 1963): 152-167. See also F. H. Bradley, *Principles of Logic* (Oxford, 1883).

"The discourse of the other...." Jacques Lacan, Seminar II, in *Le moi dans la théorie de Freud et dans la technique de la psychanalyse, 1954-1955* , Ed. Jacques-Alain Miller (Paris: Éditions du Seuil, 1978), Trans. Sylvana Tomaselli & John Forrester (Cambridge: Cambridge UP, 1988), 89.

"No terror is as total...." Jackson Mac Low, *Vort* 8 (Silver Spring, Maryland) 1975.

"The demonstrative *this*...." Ludwig Wittgenstein, *Philosophical Investigations: the English text of the third edition*, Trans. G.E.M. Anscombe (Englewood Cliffs: Prentice Hall, 1973), 45.

"Nature abhors a fact." Hume, David. *An Enquiry Concerning Human Understanding* (La Salle: Open Court, 1949): 129 et seq. *Cf.* Benedict Spinoza.

"The object of this paper...." Erik Kjær Pedersen, "Continuously Controlled Surgery Theory," in *Surveys on Surgery Theory* Volume I, *Annals of Math Studies* 145 (2000): 308.

"The equation of my language...." Robert Smithson, "The Spiral Jetty," in *The Collected Writings of Robert Smithson: Essays with Illustrations*, Ed. Nancy Holt (NY: N. Y. U. P., 1979): 114.

"Strokes I have seen...." *O. E. D.*, Vol. I, 693.

"Fall; ruin." *Ibidem*, Vol. XIV, 285.

"Let none...." Translation of MHDEIS AGEWMETRHTOS EISITW; *cf.* Joannes Philoponus: *Commentaria in Aristotelem graeca: edita consilio et auctoritate Academiae litterarum regiae borussica*. Berolini, typ. et impensis G. Reimeri, Volume XV (M. Hayduck, Berlin 1897): 117.

"August is the month of memory...." Subcomandante Marcos, communiqué from La Realidad, Chiapas (13 August, 1999).

"The next step we must take...." Aristotle, *Physics* Book IV: 210a14-210a24.

"Intuitively, (A, *a*) represents...." Pedersen, "Surgery Theory," 314.

"In one way, a finger...." Aristotle, *Physics*, Book IV: 210a14-210a24.

"One would obviously want...." Pedersen, "Surgery Theory," 313.

"Hence the fiber represents...." Pedersen, "Surgery Theory," 319.

"He who does not forget...." *A Slap in the Face of Public Taste*, Aleksei Kruchenych (Moscow, 1912).

"More generally, little importance...." Guy Debord, *Panegyric*, Volume I, Trans. James Brook (London: Verso, 1991): Chapter IV.

"A necessary yet effectively...." Aleksandra Wagner, "The Nature of Demand," in *Radical Reconstruction* (New York: Princeton Architectural Press, 1997), 10.

"If any bodye weare...." A. M. tr. Gabelhouer's *Bk. Physicke* 54/1 (1599).

"I assure you that...." Montaigne, *Essais de messire Michel seignevr de Montaigne, chevalier de l'Ordre du roy, & gentil-homme ordinaire de sa chambre* (A. Bovrdeavs: par S. Millanges, 1580).

"Then purg'd, with Euphrasie...." John Milton, *Paradise Lost: A Poem in Twelve Books, The Second Edition, Revised and Augmented* (London: S. Simmons, 1674), Book XI, ll. 414-5.

"Vectors of space that never existed." Lebbeus Woods, project notes, in *Radical Reconstruction*. Cf. David Peat, *The Philosopher's Stone*, 133.

"The last apparatus eliminates...." Erwin Panofksy, *The Life and Art of Albrecht Dürer* (Princeton: Princeton University Press, 1955), 253.

"Is falne into the Sear...." William Shakespeare, *The Tragedie of Macbeth*, Act V, s. iii, ll. 22-23.

"In the Scale of dure...." John Douland [*id est* Dowland]. [*Andreas*] *Ornithoparcus: his micrologus, or introduction: containing the art of singing* (London: Printed for Thomas Adams, 1609), translation and emendation of the 1515 original.

"But how do we know where...." Ludwig Wittgenstein, *Preliminary Studies for the 'Philosophical Investigations,' Generally Known as the Blue & Brown Books* (Oxford: Blackwell, 1969), 49.

"What signified, she said...." Sir Walter Scott, *St. Ronan's Well, or, the fatal effects of a clandestine marriage: a Scottish tale in which are displayed the villainous treachery and just punishment of the Earl of Etherington, the misfortunes of his brother, Francis Tyrell, and the barbarous treatment and cruel death of his affianced bride, Miss Clara Mobray*, Book III (London: Dean & Munday, 1824).

"And why is it that scars...." Aristotle, *Problems* Book IX: 889b20-889b26.

"Sunned at spine...." About Books, *Catalogue* (Owen Sound, Ontario, 2000), listing for E. R. Henry's *Classification and Uses of Fingerprints* (London: Routledge, 1900).

"Very occasional...." Simon Finch Rare Books, Catalogue 45 (London, 1999), listing for Sir Arthur Conan Doyle, [*The Works*], (London: Smith, Elder & Co., 1903).

"In all my doings...." Albrect Dürer, diary, mid June 1521.

Point and Line to Plane. Wassily Kandinskii. *Punkt und Linie zu Flüche:*

Beitrag zur Analyse der malerischen Elemente (München: Albert Langen, 1926), translated as *Point and Line to Plane: contribution to the analysis of the pictorial elements* (NY: Solomon R. Guggenheim Foundation for the Museum of Non-Objective Painting, 1947).

"History is the science...." ["L'histoire est la science du malheur des hommes"]. Raymond Queneau, *Une Histoire Modèle* (Paris: Gallimard, 1966), 9.

"(a name, gift; a blow, injury)." *O. E. D.*, Vol. VIII, 677.

"The meaning of a name...." Ludwig Wittgenstein, *Philosophical Grammar*, Ed. Rush Rhees and Trans. Anthony Kenny (Oxford: Blackwell, 1974), 27.

"You learned the *concept*...." Ludwig Wittgenstein, *Philosophical Investigations*.

"The profound fascination...." Walter Benjamin, *Das Passagen-Werk*, as part of *Gesammelte Schriften*, Vol. V (Frankfurt: Suhrkamp, 1982); translated by Howard Eiland and Kevin McLaughlin as *The Arcades Project* (Cambridge: Belknap, 1999).

"My hurts are constant...." Lyn Hejinian, Papers (MSS 74), Mandeville Special Collections Library, University of California at San Diego.

"The house where I live...." André Breton, *L'amor fou* (Paris: Gallimard, 1937), translated as *Mad Love* by Mary Ann Caws (Lincoln: University of Nebraska Press, 1987): 11.

"When one refuses...." Smithson, "The Spiral Jetty," 112.

"Iron rails...." The echo is by chance, but compare with Arthur Henry Adams, "The Garden Of The Sea," *Maoriland: and Other Verses*(1899).

"I had a wound here...." William Shakespeare, *The Tragedie Of Anthonie, & Cleopatra*, IV, vii, l. 8.

"Perhaps make a hinge picture." Marcel Duchamp, *Boîte-verte*, dim. var. (1934).

"He has cut a pinkt...." Sir Thomas Herbert, *A Relation of some yeares travaile, begunne anno 1626. Into Afrique and the greater Asia, especially the Territories of the Persian Monarchie: and some parts of the Orientall Indies, and Iles adjacent. Of their Religion, Language, Habit, Discent, Ceremonies, and other matters concerning them* (London: 1634).

"A Misfortune...." Author Unknown, *London and Country Brewer* (1713), absorbed into the 2nd edition by William Ellis, *The London and Country Brewer[....] To Which Is Added a Philosophical Account of Brewing Strong October Beer* (London : Printed and sold by W. Meadows, 1734).

"It is said that Titian...." Don Jusko, *Dated History of Artists and Pigments*.

Language as the hair in the mirror. See Marcel Duchamp, *Apolinère Enameled*; pencil and paint on zinc or tin plate and cardboard. 24.5 x 33.9 cm, Philadelphia Museum of Art, The Louise and Walter Arensberg Collection, 1916-7.

One and Three Chairs. Joseph Kosuth, 1965. Wooden folding chair, photographic copy of a chair, and photographic enlargement of a dictionary definition of a chair; chair, 2' 8 3/8" x 1' 2 7/8" x 1' 8 7/8"; photo panel, 3' x 2' x 1/8"; text panel, 2' x 2' 1/8". The Museum of Modern Art, New York (Larry Aldrich Foundation Fund).

"This I drew...." Albrecht Dürer, ink on prepared paper over silverpoint drawing, after 1484. Graphische Sammlung Albertina, Vienna.

"Plato still allowed...." Maurice Merleau-Ponty, "The Spatiality of One's Own Body and Motility," *Phenomenology of Perception*, translation of *Phénoménologie de la perception* (Paris: Gallimard, 1947) by Colin Smith (London: Routledge, 1962), 120.

"In fact, the perceptual...." Charles Sanders Pierce, *Collected Papers*, Ed. Arthur W. Burks (Cambridge, MA: Harvard UP, 1958), Volume VII: Science and Philosophy, section 633.

"But the trouble...." Merleau-Ponty, *Phenomenology*, 120-1.

"And here again...." Ludwig Wittgenstein, *Blue and Brown Books*, 68

A chemical analysis of tears. *Confer* Gilles Adrien, Jean-Pierre Jeunet, and Marc Caro, *La cité des enfants perdus* (35mm film, 1995).

"So now what other way...." Aristotle, *Posterior Analytics* Book II: 92b2-92b3.

"a practick way." John Woodall, *The Surgeon's Mate* 1612, reprinted in *Works* (1653) 8.

"If, in saying *I*...." Ludwig Wittgenstein, *Blue and Brown Books*, 68.

"to tear, draw." *O. E. D.*, Vol. XX, 638.

"*Felicidade, sim.*" Vinícius de Moraes, "Felicidade," in *Obra Poética* (José Aguilar Editora: Rio de Janeiro, 1968): 536-537.

"No wound is shown...." Robert Smith, "Dürer as Christ?", in *Sixteenth Century Journal*, Vol. 6, Issue 2 (Oct., 1975): 32.

"Tears can draw." John Dryden, *Pal. & Arc*; ii, 345 (1700).

"Love is essentially agape." Anders Nygren *Den kristna krlekstanken genom tiderna. Eros och Agape* (Stockholm, 1930); translated by A. G. Herbert as *Agape and Eros: A study in the Christian Idea of Love* (London: Society for Promoting Christian Knowledge, 1932): i. i. 23.

"The dure on char...." *O. E. D.*, Vol. I, 288.

"Dürer drew...." Don Jusko, *Dated History of Artists and Pigments*.

"Love is not a feeling." Ludwig Wittgenstein, *Zettel*, Ed. G. E. M. Anscombe and G. H. von Wright, Trans. G. E. M. Anscombe (Berkeley: University of California Press, 1967), 504.

"Tempus erat." Virgil, *The Aeneid*, Book II, Line 268. *Confer* Horace, *Carminium* Liber I, XXXVII.

"The action of the verb...." *O. E. D.*, *e.g.* Vol. X, 265; Vol. IV, 582 and 629.

"I and you now...." *Glossary of Linguistic Terms* (Dallas: SIL International, 1997).

"The tentative...." Joseph Leo Koerner, *The Moment of Self-Portraiture in German Renaissance Art* (Chicago: U. of Chicago Press, 1993), 242. *Confer* Werner Schmidt, "Autour de l'exposition de Dresden," in *La Gloire de Dürer*, Actes & Colloques 13, Ed. Jean Richter (Paris: Faculté des lettres et des sciences humaines de l'Université de Nice, 1974): 107-116; and "Die Seitenwunde Christi auf Dürers Selbstbildnis," in *Von Macht du Bilder*: *"Kunst und Reformation,"* Ed. Ernst Ullman (Leipzig: C.I.H.A.-Kolloquims, 1982), 216-223.

"Writing is...." Paul Mann, *Masocriticism* (Albany: State University of New York Press, 1998), 6.

"How can something be...." Wittgenstein, *Blue Book*, 32.

"Don't you know then...." Ludwig Wittgenstein, *Philosophical Investigations*, 350.

"But if one wanted...." Wittgenstein, *Zettel*, 11.

"It is therefore like a ruin....." Derrida, *Memoirs*, 65.

"This began as...." Smithson, "Spiral Jetty," 114.

"A proper name...." Charles Sanders Peirce: *Collected Papers*, Eds. Charles Hartshorne and Paul Weiss (Cambridge: Harvard UP, 1931-1935), Volume V: Pragmatism and Pragmaticism, Book I, Lecture iii, section 75.

"The last...." *O. E. D.*, e.g. Vol. IX, 601; Vol. XI, 67; Vol. XIV, 559; Vol. IV, 202; Vol. XVI 16 & 460; Vol. XVII, 534.

"I marked the place...." Saint Augustine, Bishop of Hippo, *Confessions*, Book VIII, 12 ([Rouen]: [P]ermissu Superiorum. 1620), Trans. R.-S. Pinecoffin (Harmondsworth: Penguin, 1961).

Notes and Acknowledgements

"Shift" is the result of replacing a handful of vocabulary words in the introductory chapter of a geology textbook with terms from the introductory chapter of a linguistics textbook. No further editing took place. Thanks to Paul Naylor and the editors at *Facture*, where the text appeared under the title "Tectonic Grammar" (*Facture* 3 [San Diego, 2001]), and to Gregg Biglieri and Barbara Cole for the invitation to write on the topic.

"Ar," was published in *Kiosk: a journal of poetry, poetics, and experimental prose* (Spring 2003). The final page is from the description of Robert Barry's *Inert Gas* series.

The text of "Legion" comes from the true/false questions of the first edition of *The Minnesota Multiphasic Personality Inventory* (1942).

"Strand" is dedicated to Anh Quynh Bui. The source text is *On Certainty*, Ludwig Wittgenstein's research into names and rule following, and the procedural form is based on the mesostic of John Cage and Louis Mink. Although it does not share the layout of the mesostic, it adheres to the same strict rule: between any two letters of the key-word those letters may not appear. So given the index of the dedicatee's name and the source text, I read though Wittgenstein's book until I came to the first word containing an "a" but not followed by a "n" (in this case "all"), then continued until I came to a word with a "n" neither preceded by an "a" nor followed by an "h" (in this case "when"), and then the next word with a "qu" ("queer" in this instance) and so on in succession through the text. As many words on either side of the index-letter could be included so long as they fit within the typographic spread of the page and did not violate the exclusionary index-letter rule.

"Dure" is dedicated to Alessandra Squina Santos. Thanks to Kyle Schlesinger and Cuneiform Press for his version.

Special thanks to Gregg Biglieri, Christian Bök, Mónica de la Torre, Timothy Donnelly, Kenny Goldsmith, Mike Golston, Anne Jamison, Joanna Picciotto, Claudia Rankine, Adelaide Russo, Brian Kim Stefans, Darren Wershler-Henry, and Susan Wheeler.

ROOF BOOKS

- Andrews, Bruce. **EX WHY ZEE**. 112p. $10.95.
- Andrews, Bruce. **Getting Ready To Have Been Frightened**. 116p. $7.50.
- Benson, Steve. **Blue Book**. Copub. with The Figures. 250p. $12.50
- Bernstein, Charles. **Controlling Interests**. 80p. $11.95.
- Bernstein, Charles. **Islets/Irritations**. 112p. $9.95.
- Bernstein, Charles (editor). **The Politics of Poetic Form**. 246p. $12.95; cloth $21.95.
- Brossard, Nicole. **Picture Theory**. 188p. $11.95.
- Cadiot, Olivier. **Former, Future, Fugitive**. Translated by Cole Swensen. 166p. $13.95.
- Champion, Miles. **Three Bell Zero**. 72p. $10.95.
- Child, Abigail. **Scatter Matrix**. 79p. $9.95.
- Davies, Alan. **Active 24 Hours**. 100p. $5.
- Davies, Alan. **Signage**. 184p. $11.
- Davies, Alan. **Rave**. 64p. $7.95.
- Day, Jean. **A Young Recruit**. 58p. $6.
- Di Palma, Ray. **Motion of the Cypher**. 112p. $10.95.
- Di Palma, Ray. **Raik**. 100p. $9.95.
- Doris, Stacy. **Kildare**. 104p. $9.95.
- Dreyer, Lynne. **The White Museum**. 80p. $6.
- Edwards, Ken. **Good Science**. 80p. $9.95.
- Eigner, Larry. **Areas Lights Heights**. 182p. $12, $22 (cloth).
- Gizzi, Michael. **Continental Harmonies**. 92p. $8.95.
- Goldman, Judith. **Vocoder**. 96p. $11.95.
- Gottlieb, Michael. **Ninety-Six Tears**. 88p. $5.
- Gottlieb, Michael. **Gorgeous Plunge**. 96p. $11.95.
- Gottlieb, Michael. **Lost & Found**. 80p. $11.95.
- Greenwald, Ted. **Jumping the Line**. 120p. $12.95.
- Grenier, Robert. **A Day at the Beach**. 80p. $6.
- Grosman, Ernesto. **The XULReader: An Anthology of Argentine Poetry (1981–1996)**. 167p. $14.95.
- Guest, Barbara. **Dürer in the Window, Reflexions on Art**. Book design by Richard Tuttle. Four color throughout. 80p. $24.95.
- Hills, Henry. **Making Money**. 72p. $7.50. VHS videotape $24.95. Book & tape $29.95.
- Huang Yunte. **SHI: A Radical Reading of Chinese Poetry**. 76p. $9.95
- Hunt, Erica. **Local History**. 80 p. $9.95.
- Kuszai, Joel (editor) **poetics@**, 192 p. $13.95.
- Inman, P. **Criss Cross**. 64 p. $7.95.
- Inman, P. **Red Shift**. 64p. $6.
- Lazer, Hank. **Doublespace**. 192 p. $12.
- Levy, Andrew. **Paper Head Last Lyrics**. 112 p. $11.95.
- Mac Low, Jackson. **Representative Works: 1938–1985**. 360p. $12.95, $18.95 (cloth).
- Mac Low, Jackson. **Twenties**. 112p. $8.95.

- McMorris, Mark. **The Café at Light**. 112p. $12.95.
- Moriarty, Laura. **Rondeaux**. 107p. $8.
- Neilson, Melanie. **Civil Noir**. 96p. $8.95.
- Osman, Jena. **An Essay in Asterisks**. 112p. $12.95.
- Pearson, Ted. **Planetary Gear**. 72p. $8.95.
- Perelman, Bob. **Virtual Reality**. 80p. $9.95.
- Perelman, Bob. **The Future of Memory**. 120p. $14.95.
- Piombino, Nick, **The Boundary of Blur**. 128p. $13.95.
- Prize Budget for Boys, **The Spectacular Vernacular Revuew**. 96p. $14.95.
- Raworth, Tom. **Clean & Will-Lit**. 106p. $10.95.
- Robinson, Kit. **Balance Sheet**. 112p. $11.95.
- Robinson, Kit. **Democracy Boulevard**. 104p. $9.95.
- Robinson, Kit. **Ice Cubes**. 96p. $6.
- Scalapino, Leslie. **Objects in the Terrifying Tense Longing from Taking Place**. 88p. $9.95.
- Seaton, Peter. **The Son Master**. 64p. $5.
- Sherry, James. **Popular Fiction**. 84p. $6.
- Silliman, Ron. **The New Sentence**. 200p. $10.
- Silliman, Ron. **N/O**. 112p. $10.95.
- Smith, Rod. **Music or Honesty**. 96p. $12.95
- Smith, Rod. **Protective Immediacy**. 96p. $9.95
- Stefans, Brian Kim. **Free Space Comix**. 96p. $9.95
- Tarkos, Christophe. **Ma Langue est Poétique—Selected Works**. 96p. $12.95.
- Templeton, Fiona. **Cells of Release**. 128p. with photographs. $13.95.
- Templeton, Fiona. **YOU—The City**. 150p. $11.95.
- Torres, Edwin. **The All-Union Day of the Shock Worker**. 112 p. $10.95.
- Tysh, Chris. **Cleavage**. 96p. $11.95.
- Ward, Diane. **Human Ceiling**. 80p. $8.95.
- Ward, Diane. **Relation**. 64p. $7.50.
- Watson, Craig. **Free Will**. 80p. $9.95.
- Watten, Barrett. **Progress**. 122p. $7.50.
- Weiner, Hannah. **We Speak Silent**. 76 p. $9.95
- Weiner, Hannah. **Page**. 136 p. $12.95
- Wolsak, Lissa. **Pen Chants**. 80p. $9.95.
- Yasusada, Araki. **Doubled Flowering: From the Notebooks of Araki Yasusada**. 272p. $14.95.

ROOF BOOKS
are published by
Segue Foundation, 300 Bowery, New York, NY 10012
Visit our website at **segue.org**

ROOF BOOKS are distributed by
SMALL PRESS DISTRIBUTION
1341 Seventh Avenue, Berkeley, CA. 94710-1403.
Phone orders: 800-869-7553
spdbooks.org